Hip Tranquil Chick

Hip Tranquil Chick

A Guide to Life
On and Off
the Yoga Mat

KIMBERLY WILSON

INNER OCEAN PUBLISHING
Maui • San Francisco

Inner Ocean Publishing, Inc.
P.O. Box 1239
Makawao, Maui, HI 96768-1239
www.innerocean.com

Illustrations by Morgan Johnson
Cover design by Yoori Kim
Book design by Maxine Ressler

Inner Ocean Publishing is a member of Green Press
Initiative, a nonprofit program dedicated to supporting
publishers in their efforts to reduce their use of fiber
sourced from endangered forests. We elected to print
this title on 50 percent postconsumer recycled paper
with the recycled portion processed-chlorine free. As a
result, we have saved the following resources: 32 trees,
1,521 lbs of solid waste, 11,843 gallons of water, 2,853 lbs
of net greenhouse gases, 23 million BTU's. For more
information on the Green Press Initiative, visit http://www.
greenpressinitiative.org.

PUBLISHER CATALOGING-IN-PUBLICATION DATA
Wilson, Kimberly.
    Hip tranquil chick : a guide to life on and off the yoga
    mat / Kimberly Wilson. — Maui : Inner Ocean, 2006.
        p. ; cm.
        ISBN-13: 978-1-930722-71-2
        ISBN-10: 1-930722-71-0
        1. Yoga. 2. Spiritual life. 3. Self-actualization
    (Psychology) I. Title.
B132.Y6 W55 2006
294.5/436—dc22   0611

Printed in the United States of America

06 07 08 09 10 11 DATA 10 9 8 7 6 5 4 3 2 1

DISTRIBUTED BY PUBLISHER'S GROUP WEST

For information on promotions, bulk purchases, premiums,
or educational use, please contact: 866.731.2216 or sales@
innerocean.com.

DISCLAIMER: This publication contains the opinions
and ideas of its author. The advice contained herein is
for informational purposes only. Please consult your
medical professional before beginning any diet or exercise
program, and see a financial advisor before making any
investment decisions. The author and publisher disclaim all
responsibility for any liability, loss, risk, injury, or damage
resulting from the use, proper or improper, of any of the
contents contained in this book. Every effort has been
made to ensure that the information contained in this book
is complete and accurate.

· ·

This book is dedicated to the many teachers who have

shared their wisdom with me since kindergarten, the

students I've met since my yoga teaching journey began,

my amazing team at Tranquil Space, my tranquil beau,

Tim Mooney, and my hip muse, Sir Louis the Pug.

· ·

Contents

Introduction

What lies before us and what lies behind us is

nothing compared to what lies within us.

—Ralph Waldo Emerson

Tranquil Space began not quite a decade ago in my one-bedroom apartment on the outskirts of an artsy Dupont Circle neighborhood. There was little to no yoga to be found in Washington, D.C. It was an edgy thing to do, not receiving the interest or respect it now commands. I was working as a paralegal, reading *The Artist's Way,* and seeking a more creative way of life, longing for kindred spirits, and hoping that they existed in D.C.... but how to find them?

With visions of special strangers huddled around my fireplace, drinking tea, doing yoga, and connecting, I began hanging fliers around Dupont. This was a BIG step, I realize now, but it felt so natural at the time. Inviting strangers into one's living room is not a habit I recom-

mend, but my faith in the practice of yoga and my desire for community demanded it. Surprises continued to come my way: the joy of brewing a homemade batch of chai for every class, the excitement of watching students' eyes light up when they truly felt a pose, the pleasure yoga was bringing to people who met through class, the love with which I approached the business. With a psychology degree and no clue about business, I began with a focus on the special details: ribbons wrapped around inspirational quotes that greeted the students on their mats, aromatic candles, a blazing fire to welcome students, chai served in porcelain teacups, homemade business cards and brochures. I loved putting time into making people feel nurtured. I wanted students to walk into class and feel welcomed and accepted, not judged. I especially wanted women to find a safe space to work with their bodies, develop a sense of empowerment, and realize the importance of taking steps toward their idealized life. Thus Tranquil Space began.

We have grown beyond my wildest dreams. I am constantly amazed by the sacred souls I've met, which would never have happened had I not hung up that first neighborhood flier. The reason I started the studio has been an important reflection of mine since the very first class. With the weaving together of trunk shows, vibrant studio décor, lifestyle-focused "off the mat" workshops, TranquiliT clothing collection, various charities, and my writing, I love seeing the evolution of my vision to offer more tranquility into the lives of others, particularly women.

I truly believe that yoga for the sake of yoga is powerful, but not as powerful as sprinkling it throughout one's lifestyle. Yoga serves as my catalyst, my core, that place I turn to when my world is spinning. I was drawn to it for the healing powers that it provided mentally and physically. How extraordinary to actually spend time connecting to the body, surrendering the mind, pushing the edges of comfort, while also honoring limitations!

How many of us say, "Oh, I'd love to do such and such, but now just isn't the right time"? NOW is the time to begin taking steps to create what you desire. Life is lived by stepping strategically outside one's comfort zone to head in the direction of one's dreams. This direction is not without mistakes, drama, or sometimes failure, but it is filled with authenticity because you are DOING, in addition to dreaming.

The Hip Tranquil Chick

Yoga is a lifestyle—full of mean reds, paramours, and deep twists. Hip tranquil chickness is a movement to live in a way that shines. After all, that is why we are here: to shine as brightly and boldly as possible. The mission of a hip tranquil chick is to incorporate hipness and tranquility into all aspects of life.

Hip = your external presentation: fun, fashion, frivolity.

Tranquil = your internal world: the savvy substance behind the style.

Chick = your energy: *joie de vivre*.

The hip tranquil chick is a swanky girl-on-the-go looking for some tranquility along the way. She juggles a busy life with grace, lives her practice, makes time for thoughtful gestures, gives of her resources, lights up a room with her presence. She embodies a passion for life. She lives in a mindful, conscientious manner that helps spread true tranquility. She is the girl we aspire to be.

How to Use this Book

Hip Tranquil Chick is divided into "on the mat" and "off the mat" sections. "On the mat" explains yoga philosophy with examples of modern girl scenarios where these principles can be applied, and explains the styles and benefits of yoga. This section also offers seven yoga sequences to help the modern diva cope, such as "Breathe Your Way to Tranquility" and "Energizing Sun Salutes." Instructions are geared to the most basic beginner. No yoga experience is necessary, only yoga curiosity. The "on the mat" section helps grow your understanding of yoga and its relevance to leading a full life, and shares ways to use yoga to transform a hurried, imbalanced lifestyle.

"Off the mat" explores nine ways to become more fabulously composed through taking yoga concepts, such as introspection, strength, and flexibility, into daily life. These lifestyle chapters are divided into Inner Chic, Outer Chic, and Combo Chic and reveal which fashion must-haves turn your on-the-mat wear into on-the-town style, how you can curb retail-therapy debt, how strategic soirée throwing creates community, and how you can practice social consciousness. This section addresses many modern girl situations and offers inspiring ways to live your dreams by taking small steps, asking yourself the right questions, and creating your own reality.

Each chapter ends with "Savvy Sources" to read, listen, or visit, along with supportive "Omwork" to help you explore the concepts further. This book is a tool for bringing tranquility into the various chapters of your life. Read the book from the very beginning or choose the chapters that you're most drawn to and dive in.

Think of *Hip Tranquil Chick* as the modern girl's bible to living life with a fusion of fashion, passion, and consciousness. Relish the notion that you are growing when you step onto the mat and out your front door each day. Honor the intentions and dedications that you create. Begin each day with the one-pointed focus we seek in yoga, and end each day in gratitude. Explore your unlimited

potential—the first step to embodying yoga as a lifestyle. Let your practice be as unique as you are. Embrace the teachings, hold on to what resonates with you, and continue to live your life one pose at a time. Namaste.

Hip Tranquil Chick Quiz

Hip Tranquil Chick (hip-tra[ng]-kwəl-ˈchik) n.,

A woman who weaves her practice of yoga and love of

all things fabulous into a hip and tranquil lifestyle.

Υou know you're a hip tranquil chick if you answer yes to the following:

1. Do you dream of doing big things?
2. Do you long for balance while maintaining your bustling social life?
3. Is thinking globally and serving others important to you?
4. Would you never dream of leaving home without lip gloss?
5. Is yoga, in one of its many forms, a must-have piece of your lifestyle?
6. Is creativity as important to you as breathing?
7. Are you striving to be a savvy, girly, empowered woman?
8. Are kitten heels, a long strand of faux pearls, a little black dress, and the perfect bamboo yoga pants staples in your wardrobe?
9. Do you love throwing cheap chic soirées in your swanky surroundings?
10. Is your vision to lead a mindfully extravagant life?

Hip Tranquil Chick Manifesto

Live fully, seek serenity, laugh often, tread mindfully, savor simplicity, love passionately, think globally, exude creativity, treasure tranquility.

As a Hip Tranquil Chick, I, _____ , promise to:

- create a vision for my life
- nourish my inner artist through constant creativity
- breathe through challenges
- consciously carve my career path
- host savvy soirées to expand my community
- mindfully manage my money
- design an oasis to nurture my soul at home and work
- indulge in socially conscious actions
- exude my signature style with a dash of flair
- challenge myself daily
- seek opportunity and express gratitude
- serve as an inspiration to others
- nurture my relationships daily
- surround myself with candles, flowers, and positive pals
- nourish my body with oodles of water, fresh fruit, and whole grains
- schedule herbal tea sipping, bathtub soaking, and journal writing
- find inspiration in the mundane
- practice yoga gracefully on and off the mat

I did not come to yoga

to stretch. I came to live.

—Maya Breuer

Part I

Yoga on the Mat

Yoga on the mat is where the lifestyle
practice begins for hip tranquil chicks
searching for more in their lives.
By connecting inward through the
physical practice of yoga, you begin
to see the profound effects on your
life off the mat. Let's jump in and
enjoy what unfolds.

Chapter 1

Personalized Practice

create a passionate yoga practice

. . . .

Each pose is new every day, and each

day every pose can teach something new.

—JUDITH LASATER

Itook my first yoga class a decade ago while living in the mountains of Colorado, and was immediately smitten. The concentration on breath, the encouragement to listen to my body, and the powerful poses lured me into this ancient practice. Finally, I'd found something that not only strengthened my body but also nourished my soul and helped me tame that oh-so-busy mind.

Yoga translates as "union," and that's why there is such an emphasis on the balance between the mind, body, and spirit. The practice of yoga expands well beyond the physical postures, or asanas, that it is most associated with in the West. Originating in India about five thousand years ago, this practice has become increasingly popular in the Western world, and many modern girls are turning to it to stay sane.

When the Indian sage Patanjali wrote the fundamental teachings of yoga, the Yoga Sutras, more than two thousand years ago, he emphasized that the aim of yoga is to quiet the fluctuations of the mind and to create an internal stillness. The Yoga Sutras outline meditation, practice, and philosophy, helping practitioners connect to their inner voice and find a state of balance. In this way, yoga leads to tranquility—found through reining in our busy minds and opening up our tired bodies. In today's chaotic world, who needs this more than the modern girl? We are trying to do it all, have it all, and savor a dose of spirituality at the same time.

Yoga is about balance, not abstinence. Anyone can start a yoga practice—young, old, male, female, Mormon, or Muslim. Through the practice of yoga you become more flexible and may cut down on your martini consumption, but it's all about doing things consciously and in moderation. Your yoga practice is fun and is to be enjoyed fully, just like your fabulous life.

Why Yoga?

The benefits of starting a personalized yoga practice run the gamut from getting physically toned to feeling more spiritually centered, emotionally healthy, and mentally focused. All you need to start this life-changing practice is the desire to try something new or, if you are already practicing, to incorporate yoga into a luxe lifestyle that exudes a chic consciousness. A leopard-print yoga mat or the latest form-fitting, figure-flattering yoga ensemble is not necessary—though I personally find that looking and feeling my best

> When I started doing asana, the yoga postures, I had a very strong feeling of many unnecessary things dropping away.
> —PATRICIA SULLIVAN

while practicing yoga is always a plus. What you really need is the willingness to let yoga connect to your mind and body to help you add balance and tranquility to your already very full life. Just as yoga challenges you with new poses and provides variations on old ones through the integration of the lessons learned on the mat, you develop the confidence, flexibility, and strength to challenge yourself with new experiences off the mat.

Tranquil Tip: Getting your yoga groove on may take a few minutes. Your mind may still be swirling from your whirlwind day, you may be easily distracted, and you may find the initial poses challenging. However, give it time. Once your body opens up and your mind quiets down, the practice becomes transformative. Nothing, not even good dark chocolate, beats the euphoric sensations of final relaxation!

What Is My Yoga?

To truly create a personalized practice, it is important to determine what you're seeking through yoga. Is it serenity in the city, a firm yoga bum, or enhanced spirituality? How about social time with girlfriends, improved strength, a meditation practice, increased flexibility, or all of the above? What you seek today may be very different from what you need in the future. Keep this in mind to allow for your continuous growth as a yogini. Just because you want to practice yoga now because all your girlfriends do it, or you want to whittle away at your waist, doesn't mean that your relationship with yoga won't change over time. Yoga fosters positive personal growth that extends well beyond the physical practice of poses. Sometimes you never know where it will take you.

A hip tranquil chick's approach to yoga and life is nondogmatic. There are many paths to yoga and many ways to practice yoga, and there is no need to be chained indefinitely to any particular mode of practice. You can spend time experimenting with yoga styles, knowing that your needs evolve over time. Try different teachers within the styles, pay attention to how you feel in various yoga communities, and choose what's best for you. This allows you to avoid dogmatic precepts that may make you feel caged, because, as we know, a woman needs the continued opportunity to change her mind.

Styles of Yoga in Modern Girl Terms

It is helpful to determine if you like routine or are seeking a "surprise" with each practice. One of the biggest differences between the styles of yoga is that some offer a set sequence every time, while others will vary with each class. Understanding your person-

ality and preferences will help you determine where you fit in the yoga spectrum.

Anusara means "to step into the current of divine will." Students hear phrases like "puff your kidneys" and "open to grace," and receive a practice that is spiritually inspiring while grounded in biomechanics. The class focus weaves attitude, alignment, and action. Keen attention to detail, flowery language, and demonstrations during class make this a unique and powerful style. Texan founder John Friend exudes a passion for yoga and has a rapidly growing number of devotees. For more information, visit www.anusara.com.

. . . .

I practice now not so much
with ambition as with gratitude.
—JUDITH LASATER

. . . .

Ashtanga, is a set series in a warm room that is quite vigorous and cathartic. The fast-paced primary and secondary series are those most commonly found at Ashtanga studios, although there are actually six series. The practice is for the athletic yogini who loves knowing which pose comes next while

Yoga Chick Quiz

If you're a newbie, you can figure out where to begin with this quiz, and if you're a seasoned yogini, you can expand your yogic horizons.

1. Is a set routine a must for your practice? Bikram or Ashtanga is for you.
2. Do you have to have great tunes to practice yoga? Usually vinyasa, but it varies: ask the studio or teacher.
3. Do you prefer having poses broken down, demonstrated, and moving slowly at first? Explore Anusara or Iyengar.
4. Is precision in poses very important to you? Anusara or Iyengar is a must.
5. Do you find that the more noise, bustling, and distraction around your practice, the better? Try a gym or health club over a studio.
6. Does a heated room help you unfold during practice? Bikram or Ashtanga like it hot.
7. Does receiving physical assists during yoga help your practice grow? Varies: ask the studio or teacher. Be sure to let them know if you have injuries.
8. Do you love a graceful, dancelike yoga practice? Ah ha, check out vinyasa or Ashtanga.
9. Do you enjoy seamlessness in your practice? Ashtanga or vinyasa it is!
10. Do you appreciate the teacher pushing you to go further in an authoritative way? Bikram is your bag.

floating in and out of standing and seated poses. K. Pattabhi Jois, who lives in Mysore, India, created this popular and intense style that appeals to a more Type-A crowd. For

It matters less what we do in practice than how we do it and why we do it.
—Donna Farhi

more information, visit www.ashtanga.com.

Bikram is a set series of 26 poses in 100-degree heat where the bikini-clad, microphone-wearing teachers encourage you to push harder, harder, harder. Similar to Ashtanga, it is great for students who appre-ciate knowing a sequence, love to sweat, and enjoy being challenged in an intense way. A connoisseur of Rolls-Royces, founder Bikram Choudhury lives in Los Angeles and was once coined the "bad boy of yoga" by *Yoga Journal*. For more information, visit www.bikramyoga.com.

Iyengar emphasizes precise muscular and skeletal alignment. This style will help you connect to subtle parts of your body that you didn't know you had. Classes can feel like kindergarten when they have you running to the closet to get your strap, block, blanket, or bolster. Props are used heavily in this style and help you find the perfect pose—great for those who love detail, but challenging for those who lack patience and want lots of movement. Founder B. K. S. Iyengar lives in India and is renowned in the world of yoga. His certified teachers have been through rigorous training. This style makes for a great foundation for all yoginis. For more information, visit www.bksiyengar.com.

Vinyasa (often called "flow") offers a ton of inspiration for the teacher and the student. It emerged from the roots of Krishnamacharya's (considered the grandfather of modern yoga) lineage of Ashtanga, Iyengar, and Viniyoga styles, and focuses on the linking of flowing poses with breath. If you love to dance, you'll love the graceful, challenging flow of vinyasa, with its continuous creativity. As a practitioner, I love how it translates beautifully off the mat to encourage mindful movement, breath connection, and an appreciation of life's continual ebb and flow.

What Is Hatha?

You'll often find "hatha yoga" offered at gyms. Hatha refers to the physical poses of yoga and is sometimes used generically to describe a yoga asana practice. It translates as *ha* ("sun") and *tha* ("moon")—the balance of opposites, namely, the masculine and feminine aspects that reside within us. During the practice of yoga and modern life, the hip tranquil chick seeks to balance effort and surrender. She acknowledges opposites within herself and is always looking for balance between them.

Namaste ... Do What?

You will hear this word at the end of class and may even be greeted this way. Wonder what it means? It is a gesture acknowledging the divine spark within each of us that translates as "I honor the divine within you from the divine within me." Place your hands in prayer position, feel the thumbs connect to your heart center, close your eyes, and bow your head. The modern yoga girl approaches others, who are all her teachers, with respect and honor—from her fave barista to a respected mentor.

There are many additional styles of yoga, and their number continues to grow. Experience the various styles to make an educated decision based on what works best for your body and mind. Notice that as you deepen your connection to your intuition, a vigorous practice may be appealing when you have a strong need to release pent-up energy after a challenge-filled day. In turn you'll also recognize when you crave a chill yin or restorative yoga practice. Learn to blend various styles based on your many moods.

Your yoga is a way to showcase your personal style and preferences. It is important to honor this individuality each time you step onto the mat. You will never approach your practice with the same feelings or experiences twice. Every day on the mat, like every day in life, will be new. This personalized practice is carried into all areas of your life— at home, on the go, and in the office.

Every Day, Anywhere

Yoga is an integral part of the hip tranquil chick's daily routine. By carving out a space for your practice or simply having your mat nearby, ready to be unrolled at a moment's

. . . .

The spiritual journey is the soul's
life commingling with ordinary life.
—CHRISTINA BALDWIN

. . . .

notice, you build a powerful connection with yourself and your world, every day, anywhere. We are always in motion—wandering through a museum, flirting on a date, browsing at the bookstore, sipping chai at a sidewalk café. By staying connected to our practice, we blend our busy modern lives with balance and tranquility.

Try a little tranquility-on-the-go. While waiting in the line that never seems to move, instead of letting the delay get to you and succumbing to a hissie fit, shift your weight

onto one leg and place the other foot on the opposite ankle to practice the tranquility-invoking tree pose. During that yawn-inducing staff meeting, excuse yourself for a moment. Hide out in the loo for a few minutes to do some twists, forward folds, and shoulder openers to return refreshed. With the principles of yoga internalized and practiced spontaneously, you'll find a sense of peace within everyday life's pandemonium.

Yoga Class Prep

The essentials for class are a yoga mat, comfy clothes, a hand towel, and bottled water. You may be able to rent a yoga mat or hand towel if you don't have your own. Wear clothes that stretch and flatter, and be sure to dress in layers so that as the body warms and cools throughout the practice, you have the pieces nearby. Black pants, camis with built-in support, and wrap tops are great for class, and transition fabulously to and from pre- and postpractice events.

Arrive to class with an open heart, receptive to what you are about to experience. Be on time, especially if you are new to the studio, so you can get your bearings. If you do arrive late due to a delayed train or a dress fitting that ran over, be sure to cause as little disruption as possible to the yogis already in their zone. Bring a beginner's mind to your practice and let go of expectations or preconceptions. Enjoy being in your body as if it were the first time you are experiencing such bliss.

Practice for Perfect Tranquility

How often should you practice? Ideally, every single day. However, when you first begin, at least a weekly practice is recommended to establish a routine. As your yoga experience grows, a daily practice is encouraged, even if only for a few minutes. Try to carve out a minimum of five minutes each day for at least a forward fold or down dog. Notice how your body begins to crave the practice and your muscles actually ache for it.

On-the-Mat Practice = In-Your-Life Perks

Transform on-the-mat lessons to off-the-mat success. In addition to these tangible benefits, yoga stimulates a powerful and seemingly unconscious desire for more mindful and healthy life habits. For example, you may find yourself sipping herbal tea instead of gulping espresso, breathing deeply instead of chain-smoking, seeking time for reflection instead of consuming cosmos at happy hour, involving your mind along with your body during exercise in a space that feels sacred instead of vacantly working the StairMaster in a techno-pumping gym, and surrounding yourself with positive and supportive companionship. Yoga expands beyond the yoga mat—it begins to seep into your lifestyle, transforming you one pose at a time.

Benefit	On the Mat	Off the Mat
Increased confidence	After several attempts, you lift up into a headstand	You finally ask for that raise at work
Improved body awareness	You are able to find your edge without moving past it into injury	You are aware of how outside stimuli affect you, including food, people, and situations
Graceful movement	You feel as if you're dancing in vinyasa class	You walk into a room with poise
An opportunity to slow down and take a break from life	You savor your practice time as an escape from the ordinary	You are able to return to a tranquil space while on the go through tips learned in yoga
A community filled with spiritually minded people	You meet girlfriends who share a passion for yoga	Your yoga buddies may also have a passion for fun
A connection to breathing that helps you get grounded even in sticky situations	When stuck in scorpion pose, this comes in very handy	When stuck in a bad date, this is doubly handy
Improved sleep patterns	Translates as more energy for yoga	And even more energy for life
A deeper connection to your inner voice and intuition	Your yoga practice evolves based on your personal style and needs	You make choices based on this deeper infusion of inner knowing

Tranquility through Community

To find the perfect place to practice yoga, research various studios and teachers in your area. Ask for recommendations, search the Internet, and peruse local publications for yoga studios. Try a few places on for size until the right fit emerges. Look for a place where you feel comfortable and fabulous, where the ambience is inviting, and where you can see yourself and your practice growing. You may also find a new haven of spiritually minded girlfriends to sip soy lattes with after class. Many students rave that the studio has become their "church"—a home for seeking serenity and inspiration in today's harried world. Your yoga community can become a true base for tranquility.

> ## Enhance Your Postflow Glow
>
> Luxury items for the hip chick's yoga bag are **moist towelletes** to freshen up before heading out and about, rosewater facial **hydrating mist** (recipe in chapter 5), **rosebud salve** (glosses lips, controls hair frizzies, and soothes dry skin all in one little tin), and **white musk** perfume oil to dab behind the ears. Voilà! You're refreshed and ready to transition to the town.

. . . .

The real act of discovery is
not in finding new lands, but
in seeing with new eyes.
—MARCEL PROUST

. . . .

Tranquil Tip: When practicing in the heart of a bustling city or a heavily trafficked strip mall in the suburbs, you may find it hard to settle in initially. The goal is to let go of all distractions, both external (honking horns, voices outside, traffic) and internal (self-talking, creating to-do lists, recapping the day), and to turn your awareness to your breath. Let everything else go.

The Connection Within

As you progress in your practice of yoga on and off the mat, notice how you become keenly aware of your body. Although your yoga teacher's continued requests to scoop your tailbone, open your heart center, and blossom your sitting bones may seem peculiar at first, eventually you become acquainted with the most subtle parts of your physical form. The simple recognition of how you feel after eating something, or after interacting with someone, allows you to make healthier decisions that align with your core values. After succumbing to my overactive sweet tooth, I notice an energy spike followed by lethargy. Whereas if I indulge in whole grains and veggies, I lack the guilt and keep an even-keeled energy level. The time spent tuning in to your body also helps release your overactive mind and ease your stress. Yoga helps you learn to slow down, even in the midst of daily drama that may compel you to pick up the pace. By making the time for yoga on a regular basis, you will be able to replenish your inner well, gain energy, and connect to your intuitive side.

 **Tranquil Tip:** Tune out of your mind and in to your body. Take time to disconnect from routine, even for only a moment. Begin with centering. Simply close your eyes and notice your breath. Inhale and exhale deeply and fully. Notice sensations throughout your body—heartbeat, heat, coolness, tightness, openness. Bring awareness to emotions—anger, anxiety, excitement, concern, sadness. Devote a piece of your week to activities that help you lose track of time, cares, and concerns—yoga, gardening, cooking, writing, dancing.

Yoga supports living with authenticity, awareness, and alignment. Regular reflection, meditation, and yoga practice allow you to connect more deeply to who you really are. This inner connection ultimately helps you make healthy, value-based decisions to move forward in life. Connect these concepts with your values and passions, and you become more proactive and less reactive. Your relationships improve and your state of mind is enriched because you are now able to find a calm port in life's sea of chaos. By spending time connecting within, you explore your authentic self, what you really want, and where you are going on this exciting journey called life. Learn to use this newfound insight and self-awareness to create a passion-filled existence that exudes a chic and spiritual consciousness. Pull out your colorful yoga mat, light a candle, put on some chill music, dress in your favorite yoga togs, and watch a world of possibility unfold.

Omwork

Try Iyengar, vinyasa, Anusara, Bikram, and Ashtanga classes to fully experience the variations among these styles. Write about your experience: how you felt after the practice, what aspects appealed to you, what aspects you disliked, what music was used, what ambience was created, and ultimately how you emerged postpractice.

Practice your yoga during challenging situations such as asking for a raise, requesting better performance from an employee, confronting a friend who has hurt you, or any other situation that makes you squeamish. Stand tall in mountain pose, approach the situation with compassion, connect with your breath, weave strength for your perspective with flexibility for theirs, speak your truth, and detach from the outcome.

Start a yoga journal. In addition to writing down how certain styles of yoga work for you, begin to write out how your continued practice feels for you. What were your emotions before you began practicing? How did you feel after practicing? Have you noticed progress in your poses or are you feeling sluggish? Use this journal to record your physical practice of yoga, along with your everyday practice of yoga off the mat.

Savvy Sources

Read

Living Yoga: A Comprehensive Guide for Daily Life, by Georg Feuerstein

The Woman's Book of Yoga and Health: A Lifelong Guide to Wellness, by Linda Sparrowe and Patricia Walden

Light on Yoga, by B. K. S. Iyengar

Living Yoga: Creating a Life Practice, by Christy Turlington

Fit Yoga magazine

Simple Living magazine

Visit

www.hiptranquilchick.com/blog

www.yogasite.com

www.yogafinder.com

www.yogajournal.com

www.yoga.com

Listen

Music for Slow Flow Yoga, by Gabrielle Roth & The Mirrors

Adagio: Music for Yoga, by Peter Davison

Sundari: A Jivamukti Yoga Class, by Gabrielle Roth & The Mirrors

Yoga Chill: Global Sounds for Yoga and Meditation, by various artists

Green Tea: Flavored Atmosphere, by various artists

Worlds Within, by Govinda

Chapter 2

Sensational Sequences

7 yoga sequences for the hip chick

· ·

When we practice asana we have the chance to bring our attention

to here and now, to the sensations and awareness we are feeling.

—JUDITH LASATER

These 30 poses will help the hip tranquil chick get her tranquility on. Combine them in the numerous proposed suggestions or play with a pose one at a time, and reap unlimited benefits when adding them to your daily repertoire.

1. reclined twist

2. four-limbed staff pose

3. staff pose

4. plank pose

5. cobra pose

variation: up dog

6. mountain pose

7. lunge

8. down dog

9. legs-up-the-wall
*variations: wide-legged V
and bent knees*

10. seated twist

11. warrior 1

12. warrior 2

13. reverse warrior

14. side angle pose

15. triangle

16. tree pose

17. bridge pose

*variations: add block under sacrum
or lift into wheel*

18. pigeon pose

19. blanket under spine

20. double pigeon pose

21. half-split

22. down dog split

23. reclined butterfly pose
variations: with blanket under spine vertically and horizontally

24. yogic squat

25. seated forward fold

26. standing forward fold

27. chair pose

28. child's pose

29. table pose

30. relaxation

Open Body, Open Mind

The key to living a tranquil life begins with being in touch with your body and understanding its close connection to your mind and overall well-being. Dance legend Martha Graham once proclaimed, "There is a vitality, a life force, a quickening that is translated through you into action.... You have to keep open and aware directly to the urges that motivate you." For a modern girl in a fast-paced society, it can be challenging to balance personal, professional, psychological, and spiritual needs. Yoga is a tool that helps bring synergy to these various components.

This chapter offers seven sequences that will help today's on-the-go gal cope with everyday life. Choose a sequence to suit your mood. Have fun with it. Breathe in self-compassion while breathing out negativity. Let yourself go.

Sequence 1: Breathe Your Way to Tranquility

This sequence can help you shine during the highly anticipated annual review, at the awkward company picnic, in a long line at the yoga studio, on a date with Not-So-Fabulous, squished on a city bus, or on a turbulent airplane. The following **three-part yoga breath** will help bring you into a state of tranquility.

Set the stage. Shift awareness to your breath and away from the situation. Is the breath fast, shallow, slow, or smooth? Notice each inhalation and exhalation. Without making judgments or altering the breath, simply observe your sensations. This will help you tune out the challenging stimulus—or person. Notice all the sensations in your body, feelings of heat or coolness, tightness or openness. With your inhalation, draw in a sense

Create a Sacred Yoga Space

Carve out enough space for your mat. Turn your cell phone to "vibrate." Put on tunes that correspond with the energy of the practice you've chosen (chill tunes for a restorative session, up-tempo beats for energizing sun salutes). Dim the lighting. Have any necessary props nearby (blankets, straps, blocks). Light a candle or incense. Hang a Do Not Disturb sign on the door if you don't live alone. Put on your most comfy, clingy, and stylish yoga gear. Pull your hair back with a sequined headband, or put it into a ponytail or funky bun. Remove bracelets or watches. Feel free to keep on your chandelier earrings if they don't get in the way and help you feel glamorous while getting your yoga on.

of relaxation, self-compassion, and inner strength. Notice anything weighing heavy on you. Visualize your cares and concerns releasing with your exhalation.

Deepen the breath. After a minute or so of being aware of the breath pattern, focus on your inhalation. Count silently as you draw the breath in: one, two, three, four. Exhale: one, two, three, four. Close your mouth. Relax your jaw and tongue. Soften the space between your eyebrows. Take long, slow, fluid breaths in and out of the nose.

Find your three parts. After a couple of minutes taking full four-count breaths, draw the breath into the belly, up into the ribcage, and finally into the chest. Now exhale from the top down, beginning with the chest, ribcage, and belly. Nonchalantly (so as not to draw attention from your date or boss), place your hands on each of these three parts of the body. Bring awareness into the belly, ribcage, and chest to ensure the breath is flowing fully here.

The **three-part yogic breath** assists you in overcoming the body's automatic fight-or-flight response while allowing you the opportunity to turn within, slow down, and recharge at any time throughout your day. Breathe fully and feel fabulous.

Tranquil Tip: Notice if you're having trouble getting the breath past the upper chest and into the lungs or belly. The belly breath tends to be the hardest for many hip chicks, so I encourage you to play with this throughout your day. That way you can go right into it without much effort when you need it most. When your e-mail bell chimes or your cell phone rings, take a moment to notice your breath, bring it into your belly, and then respond to your admirer.

Sequence 2: Healing Hip Openers

This delightful sequence offers a dose of tranquility even when you get upsetting news, feel tightly wound, have back-to-back travel, are caught up in hectic holidays, or just sit all day long. Even the hippest tranquil chick has those days when just getting out of bed can be a feat. So, rather than wallowing in the "woe is me" mode, head to your yoga mat and dive into the emotional release only a hip-focused practice can give.

1. Begin in **table pose.** Take the hips to the right and make circles with the hips and torso. Repeat a few times to work out all the kinks.

2. Return to table pose, bring your knees back a couple of inches, curl your toes under, and lift your hips to **down dog,** an inverted V.

3. Inhale and lift your right leg to a **down dog split.**

4. Exhale and place your right foot in between your hands to a **lunge.** Take small rocking motions back and forth to awaken the hips. Drop your left knee, hook your thumbs, and sweep your arms overhead alongside your ears.

5. Release your hands back to the mat, pull your hips back, and straighten your right leg into a **half-split.** Flex your front foot and wiggle it forward to fully open up the back of your right leg.

6. Return to your **lunge.**

7. Exhale back with the right leg to **down dog.**

8. Gently place the right knee in between your hands for **pigeon pose,** fold forward and take 10 deep breaths. Walk your hands back to your body and lift your torso.

9. Sweep the left leg forward, place the left foot to the outside of the right knee for a **seated twist.** Extend your right arm along your ear and place the right elbow to the outside of your left knee, cartwheel the left arm behind you and gaze lovingly over your left shoulder. For a variation, internally rotate your right arm under the left knee, and bring your left arm behind your back to bind with the right. Inhale to lengthen, exhale to twist deeper. Take a

few breaths here. Return to the center to feel the difference between both sides.

10. Place your left shin on top of your right shin, and fold forward into **double pigeon.** Take 10 deep three-part yogic breaths. Gently roll up and over onto your hands and knees.

11. Return to **table pose** circles, and repeat the series on your left side.

12. End in **yogic squat.** Close your eyes, and savor the sensations washing over your body.

Tranquil Tip: Have a blanket nearby to place under your dropped knee in half-splits, under the hip of the bent leg in pigeon, or under the sitting bones in double pigeon. This helps relieve discomfort while allowing you to drop deeper into the pose with ease.

Sequence 3: Negativity-Releasing Heart Openers

Heart openers infuse the body with compassion when you experience sadness or loss, you've met a grueling deadline, you had a long drive, or you're simply congested. Some days leave that oh-so-heavy feeling in your heart center. When this happens, breathe deeply and mindfully to help counter the tense sensations. If you are able to take the breathing further by adding movement, you're well on your way to recovering from the heavy humdrum that can cloud any modern girl's modus operandi when she's pushed to certain limits. Use this sequence to jump-start your heart to a more open path.

1. Begin in **child's pose** with your big toes together and knees open. Drop your belly and chest in between your knees. Connect with your three-part breath and soften.

2. Slowly slide along the floor into **cobra pose.** Lift through the heart, soften the shoulders, and take deep, slow breaths.

3. Pull your hips up and back to **down dog.**

4. Pivot your left heel down and in, step your right foot toward your hands, lift your torso over your hips and your arms alongside the ears to **warrior 1.**

5. Lower your left arm to your left leg and lift your right arm alongside your right ear to **reverse warrior.**

6. Cartwheel your arms around to a **lunge.**

7. Step back to **down dog.**

Repeat on other side.

8. Drop your knees and lower to **child's pose.** Take 10 deep breaths. Fill the back of your body with breath.

9. Roll up to a seated pose, drop your hips to the left, extend your legs straight out, and roll down onto your back. Bend your knees, draw the heels up toward the bum so you can brush your heels with the tips of your fingers. Inhale and lift your hips up. Roll onto your shoulders, and interlace your hands underneath your body for **bridge pose.** For a variation, place a block under your sacrum, or place your hands on the mat along your ears with your fingers pointing toward your feet to lift up to **wheel pose.** Take 5 to 10 deep breaths. Roll down one vertebra at a time. Hug the knees into your chest and roll from side to side to massage your lower back.

10. End in a supported pose on your back with a blanket under the spine horizontally or vertically. Ahhh, **relaxation.**

Tranquil Tip: Reduce compression in your lower back during these heart openers by scooping your tailbone and arching the upper and middle back while simultaneously lengthening the lower back. Feel your shoulder blades draw in and down to help open and expand your heart center into these poses and in everyday life. This will help you exude an air of confidence and grace.

Sequence 4: Energizing Sun Salutes

This sequence offers a daily dose of adrenaline and is sure to revitalize when you have low energy, don't have time for a full practice, or want to start the day off with a boost. Do you ever find that when you wake up on a chilly, dark morning, you'd rather pull your lavender eye pillow back over your eyes than leap out of bed into the unknown? Well, look no further than this centuries-old series that is sure to bring pep to your step.

1. Ground yourself in **mountain pose** at the top of the mat. Feel the feet planted firmly into the earth. Press into all four corners of the feet and reach the crown of the head toward the heavens. Exhale and place your hands to prayer position in front of your heart. Inhale and extend your arms along your ears.

2. Exhale and swan-dive your arms out to the sides into a **forward fold.**

3. Inhale and step your right leg back to a **lunge.** Lift onto your fingertips to create more length in the sternum. Wiggle your right foot back so that your heel is directly over the ball of the foot, and gently rock forward and back. Breathe into your hips.

 4. Exhale and step back with your left leg to **down dog.** Press the floor away from you.

 5. Inhale and bring your shoulders over your wrists, and your heels above the balls of your feet to **plank pose.** Feel the body pulled taut in two directions.

 6. Exhale and slide your shoulder blades down your back. Bend the arms, and hug the elbows into your body so they point directly behind you as you hover over your mat. Keep the shoulder heads and hips in a straight line for **four-limbed staff pose.**

 7. Inhale and drop your belly as you slide up to **cobra pose.** Relax your shoulders from your ears.

8. Exhale, curl your toes under, and lift your hips up to **down dog.**

 9. Inhale and step forward with your right foot. Sink deeper into your **lunge** with your exhalation. Gently rock forward and back to bring life to the hips.

 10. Exhale and step your left foot to meet the right foot as you lower into a **forward fold.**

 11. Inhale, lift your torso and extend your arms out to the sides, and up alongside the ears with the palms of your hands together above your head. Exhale, lower your hands to prayer, and return to **mountain pose.** Gaze lovingly at your hands and repeat energizing series five times.

 Tranquil Tip: Throughout your sun-saluting journey, play with the constantly opposing forces—lifting arms above the head while softening the shoulders, pressing forward with your shin in a lunge while pulling back with the opposite heel, grounding into the floor with your hands while lifting your hips up into the air in down dog. Finding ease in opposition assists you well beyond the yoga mat.

Sequence 5: Stabilizing Standing Poses

Look no further than this sequence when you feel unable to focus, need to make an important decision, feel unsteady, or need a quick jolt of power or confidence to "be on." If time is of the essence, indulge in just a couple of the poses rather than the full series. The warrior poses are sure to help you approach situations with a sense of pride and fearlessness.

1. Begin in **mountain pose.**

2. Bend your knees, sweep the arms up alongside the ears, and sink your hips into **chair pose.**

3. Exhale and swan-dive to a **forward fold.**

4. Inhale and step your right foot back to a **lunge.**

5. Exhale, then step your left foot back to **down dog.**

6. Inhale, pivot your left heel down and in so that your toes are pointing to the upper left corner of your mat, bring your right foot toward your hands, lift your torso over your hips, and sweep your arms alongside your ears to **warrior 1.**

7. Exhale and extend your arms out to the sides and open your hips to **warrior 2.**

8. Lower your left arm to your left leg and extend your right arm alongside your right ear to **reverse warrior.**

9. Lower your right hand to the outside of your right foot, and extend your left arm along your left ear for **side angle pose.**

10. Straighten your right leg and lift your torso up as you reach with your right arm as far as you can, and lower your right hand to your right shin to **triangle pose.** Extend the left arm straight up and gaze at your left thumb.

11. Cartwheel the arms around to a **lunge.**

12. Step back to **down dog.**

13. Walk or jump your feet in between your hands and raise yourself up to **mountain pose.**

14. Shift your weight onto your left foot and place the right foot at the inner left thigh for **tree pose.** Bring your hands to prayer position in front of your heart, and breathe. Take 10 deep breaths. Repeat on other side.

Tranquil Tip: Put on your favorite high-energy tunes for this practice. Let the sequence flow in a dancelike fashion. Stay mindful of your knee over the ankle in warrior 1, 2, reverse warrior, and side angle. Flow with your breath. Feel a sense of empowerment flood the body. Think of this as your rock star sequence.

Sequence 6: Rejuvenating Poses

When you're jet-lagged, on your moon cycle, exhausted, coping with harried holidays, or recovering from a not-so-fab day, this sequence will become your most comforting and supportive companion. Some days (or moments) are best spent succumbing to lethargy or countering neurotic busyness with rest and relaxation into yoga. Be sure to set the stage by turning off the ringer, surrounding yourself with soothing scents and tunes, and having your silk eye pillow, lavender pulse-point cream, and blankets nearby.

1. Begin lying on your back with your **legs extended up a wall.** If your hamstrings feel snug, move your bum away from the wall a few inches to make the pose as comfy as possible. Arm variations include (a) extending the arms out to the sides with the palms facing up, (b) reaching overhead to grasp opposite elbows, and (c) placing your hands on your belly to observe your breathing. For leg **variations,** open your feet to a wide V, or bend the knees and place the soles of the feet together. Spend 3 to 15 minutes in each of these poses. Roll to your right side and up to a seated position.

2. Come to **child's pose** and place a couple of double-folded blankets or a bolster between your knees so that your torso can release into it. Keep your big toes together and open your knees wide; turn your head to either side. Breathe here for 1 to 5 minutes. Slowly lift up and slide onto your back.

3. Bring the soles of the feet together in front of your body, drop the knees open, and relax your arms out to the sides in **reclined butterfly pose.** Variations include (a) relaxing over a rolled blanket placed lengthwise along the spine with the bum on the floor, and (b) placing the blanket horizontally under your bra line at the base of your shoulder blades and letting your shoulders drop to the floor as your arms extend out to the side. Breathe here 1 to 5 minutes.

4. Remove any blankets from under the spine and place one under your knees, let your body lie flat on the mat, and extend the arms to the sides of the torso with the palms facing up. Let the feet splay open, and breathe in deep **relaxation.** Stay here for 5 to 15 minutes.

Tranquil Tip: For a variation on **legs up the wall,** place a folded blanket under your hips to elevate them. I once read that this is an Ayurvedic way to get a facial. During restorative poses, the challenge is to let go over the blankets and into the poses. You should feel sensation but never pain. If you feel strong discomfort, come out of the pose and explore ways to tone it down by not rolling the blanket fully, using a smaller blanket, spending less time in the pose initially, or alternating between the variations offered. Let your focus turn to your breath. Soften fully. Exhale tension.

Sequence 7: Detoxifying Seated Poses and Twists

Weave this sequence into your repertoire when you're ill, hung-over, angry, tired from travel, or feeling foggy. If you begin to feel a little achy and sense an oncoming cold, if you overindulged in your grandmother's pecan pie, or if you want to release tension in your lower back, look no further than this simple yet delightful sequence. As with all poses, and especially with this sequence, give yourself at least two to three hours after eating before you practice.

1. Begin in **staff pose** and flex your feet as if you had your feet pressed against a wall. Roll the flesh from the thighs, and feel your sitting bones press into the floor. Activate your legs and keep your spine straight.

2. Bend your left knee and place the sole of the foot at the inner right thigh—think of **tree pose sitting down.** Inhale, extend the arms along your ears. Exhale as you fold forward. Take a gentle twist to the right so that your body folds over that right leg. While your hands reach for the right foot, use each inhalation to lengthen the spine, and each exhalation to fold. Lengthen the chin to the shin. Hold for 30 seconds to 1 minute. Repeat on the other side.

3. Roll up one vertebra at a time. Extend the right leg to **staff pose,** roll the flesh from the thighs, and ground your sitting bones.

4. Inhale and extend the arms alongside the ears. Exhale and hinge forward from your hips. Lengthen all the way down to a **forward fold.** Bring your hands to your feet or shins. Inhale as you lengthen; exhale as you fold. Take 10 deep breaths here. Roll up slowly and bring your shoulders over your hips.

5. Place the right foot to the outside of the left knee. Bend your left knee and place the left foot to the outside of the right hip. Inhale, extend your left arm alongside your ear, and place the left elbow to the outside of the right knee. Exhale as you cartwheel the right arm behind you for a **seated twist.** For a variation, internally rotate your left arm under the right knee, and bring your right arm behind your back to bind with the left. Inhale as you lift; exhale as you twist. Take 5 deep breaths and repeat on the other side.

6. Roll down onto your back, hug your knees into your chest and rock from side to side massaging your kidneys and lower back through this gentle, detoxifying movement. Extend your right leg out, reach for your left knee with your right hand and pull it across your body. Turn your head to the left and extend your left arm out for **reclined twist.** Take 10 deep breaths and repeat on the other side.

Tranquil Tip: When coming into a forward fold, notice if you're hinging from your hips or your waist. If you find that your spine is rounding or your hinge is coming from where your wrap dresses' sash would be and your pelvis isn't tilting, elevate your bum onto a folded blanket or block to help encourage an automatic tilt.

Mixin' and Matchin'

When you have more time and would like to focus on a couple of the sequences, here are some ideas on combinations that are sure to help you get your yoga groove on:

1. **Sequence 4 + 5 + 7 = a recipe for stoking the inner fires and detoxifying.** Best practiced with energetic and motivating tunes such as hip-hop, rock, and pop with Nag Champa incense burning nearby.

2. **Sequence 1 + 2 + 6 = a recipe for going deeper in a reflective fashion.** Soft, comfy clothes coupled with jazz, chill, or lounge tunes plus a lavender silk eye pillow, make for a perfect concoction.

3. **Sequence 2 + 3 + 7 = a recipe for releasing toxins and opening the heart.** Have tissues and your journal nearby as this combination can open up blocked emotions and make for a cathartic release. Listen to the sound of your breath and let go into the poses.

4. **Sequence 4 + 3 + 6 = a recipe for strengthening and softening fusion.** Begin with upbeat pop music, then take it down to chill and finally instrumental for this all-encompassing practice.

A Yogic State of Mind

These sequences bring respite from the challenges that surround the hip tranquil chick. By carving out just a few minutes to do the three-part yogic breath throughout your day, you bring a sense of tranquility into your numerous commitments, relationships, and social settings.

By spending time in your body you will recognize patterns, be able to move through anxiety, and truly feel what is happening inside. We all encounter drama; it is how you handle the drama that sets you apart. Take the time to sequence your life strategically, both on and off the yoga mat, and watch a world of possibility open up. When you've been pushed beyond your edge, set up your sacred yoga space, and let yourself be absorbed by the flow of these powerful sequences. Living in a yogic state of mind brings tranquility to your hips, your heart, and ultimately your life.

Omwork

Practice, practice, practice. Play the observer to your varied moods. Roll out your yoga mat, play with the suggested sequence associated with your feelings, and watch what happens. Write about this in your journal. Let yourself become more proactive, rather than reactive, to life's challenges. Infuse each day with at least 10 minutes of yoga.

Choose your most challenging pose. For many hip chicks it is the four-limbed staff pose due to struggles with upper-body strength. For others it may be double pigeon pose due to those oh-so-tight hips. Either way it is time to embrace the pose and take it deeper by playing with it at least 2 to 5 minutes each day. In your journal, note any changes you observe.

Choose your most yummy pose. Yes, it's important to nurture in addition to challenge, so spend some extra time in legs-up-the-wall, child's pose, pigeon pose, or even relaxation. When the going gets tough, spend at least 5 to 10 minutes in your fave pose. Life is sure to lighten when you allow yourself this necessary and well-deserved treat.

Savvy Sources

Read

OM Yoga Today: A Yoga Practice for 5, 15, 30, 60, and 90 Minutes, by Cyndi Lee

Relax and Renew: Restful Yoga for Stressful Times, by Judith Lasater

Ashtanga Yoga: The Practice Manual, by David Swenson

Journey into Power: How to Sculpt Your Ideal Body, Free Your True Self, and Transform Your Life with Yoga, by Baron Baptiste

Yoga to the Rescue: Remedies for Real Girls, by Amy Luwis

Visit

www.kripalu.org

www.eomega.org

www.abc-of-yoga.com

Listen

Vinyasa Yoga for the Newbie Yogi, by Kimberly Wilson

Vinyasa Yoga with Kimberly Wilson

Get Your Yoga On, by Kimberly Wilson

Yoga Sanctuary: A Guided Hatha Yoga Practice, by Shiva Rea

The Yogi's Companion, by Lauren Peterson

Chapter 3

Moral Code Musings

yoga philosophy in modern girl lingo

. . . .

Yoga changes the way you feel, the way you look

at things, and the way you interpret what's going on.

—Erich Schiffmann

Hip tranquil chicks find ways to blend yoga with their oh-so-busy lifestyle to create an overall feeling of tranquility. By practicing the eightfold path of *ashtanga,* you embody your yoga and, ultimately, live a tranquil life. In Sanskrit,

. . . .

Vogue and *Self* are putting out
the message of yoginis as buff
and perfect. . . . Most people
get beyond that and see that
it's much, much more.
—Patricia Walden

. . . .

ashtanga means "eight limbs" (*ashta* = eight, *anga* = limb), and is easily confused with the Ashtanga *style* of yoga. However, the eightfold *path* of yoga is a tool for creating a meaningful, healthy, and rewarding existence for the modern girl.

Eight Steps to Enlightenment

The eight limbs of *ashtanga* provide direction for moral and ethical behavior, offer awareness of one's overall health, provide a compass for decision making, and encourage the hip tranquil chick to find ways to express herself as a mindful maven in all she does. Best of all, they're designed so you can explore them at your own pace, one step at a time.

Step 1. The ethical foundation of the path is a list of **yogic don'ts.** These range from basic precepts such as not stealing or lying to more subtle manifestations, including shopping moderately and following your intuition. The five foundational principles, or restraints (*yamas*), are nonviolence (*ahimsa*), truth (*satya*), nonstealing (*asteya*), moderation (*brahmacharya*), and nongreed (*aparigraha*). The hip tranquil chick strives to embody these attitudes and avoids negative thoughts and actions in her daily routine.

Step 2. The next step, **yogic dos,** helps balance out the don'ts by offering alternatives to negative behaviors. These are purity (*saucha*), contentment (*samtosha*), austerity (*tapas*), study of self (*svadhyaya*), and devotion to God (*isvara pranidhana*). This step, named *niyamas,* or observances, includes actions and attitudes you cultivate to reduce suffering, while coming to see life more holistically, focusing on the bigger picture. Think of steps 1 and 2 as the Hip Tranquil Chick Commandments.

Step 3. *Asana,* the third step, translates as "seat," and consists of the **physical poses** you practice while on the yoga mat. These poses are a terrific tool to help release your overactive mind to tune in to your body. The stillness encourages separation from thoughts and never-ending to-do lists. The physical practice of poses, according to Patanjali's Yoga Sutras, should be practiced with comfort and ease. The Sutras remind us to remain calm in the midst of challenge—whether we're turned upside down and twisting or faced with a giant pile of paperwork containing urgent deadlines. The point is to seek stillness in activity, and ease in difficulty. If you find yourself struggling, remind yourself that yoga should challenge you past your comfort zone, which discourages stagnation, but not past your edge, which can cause pain or injury. Life is a series of finding your edge.

Step 4. The control of your **breath, or life energy** (*prana*), is another important component on the yogic path. In yoga, breath is a symbol of life, and you can manage your energy through breath awareness. When your breath becomes shallow and your body moves into a fight-or-flight response, take a moment, slow and steady your breathing, and draw in the nectar of life you find there. This step of yoga, called *pranayama,* is great for the tranquility tool kit and helps when you're waiting in lines, facing fears, and trying to dial down.

 **Tranquil Tip:** Alternate nostril breathing helps bring balance within, increases oxygen and energy levels, and calms the nerves. Begin by closing your right nostril with the thumb of your right hand as you inhale deeply through your left nostril, then close your left nostril with your ring finger as you exhale through your right nostril. Inhale through your right nostril, close it with your thumb, and exhale through your left nostril. Continue this pattern with deep, full, slow breaths for a few minutes and watch your mood shift.

Step 5. The next stage along the path, called *pratyahara,* is the **withdrawal of the senses.** This allows you to participate in a hectic world without always reacting to it. This principle will also help you step back, observe yourself by disengaging from the world, and help you recognize patterns that are hindering your growth. *Pratyahara* allows you to shop during a bustling holiday sale, or wait in a long line at the movie theater without getting caught up in the chaos.

The remaining three steps make up the innermost hip tranquil chick quest and are more subtle aspects of yoga practice. These subtleties allow you to control your thoughts in a way that assists you both personally and professionally. All actions stem from thought, so the ability to tighten your thought processes has profound results.

Step 6. Concentration is the ability to be fully present, to be completely in the moment and focused on only one thing. In a culture that respects multitasking, practicing concentration can be a challenge. Work to find a balance between being connected and present to each task at hand while also being efficient. Recognize when you feel frazzled, and remedy it by taking time out, regrouping, and gaining composure, rather than worrying about the future. Your ability to fully concentrate on one thing by using your breath, sensations, a mantra, or an image, is termed *dharana* and prepares for the next step of yoga.

Step 7. When you reach *dhyana,* the next step on the yogic path, you have developed a deep connection to stillness through **medi-tation.** By sitting still and tuning inward, you are quickly reminded just how busy your "monkey mind" is—full of overactive thoughts like a monkey swinging from limb to limb in a crowded forest. Stop to notice the mind's chatter and release attachment to those thoughts—practice being an observer and let them happen without holding on to them or pushing them away. This allows you to connect deeply to the internal workings of your mind, soul, and ultimately your life. When you are in a state of meditation, you are able to be completely present without having to use the tools needed in concentration. You may feel the beginnings of this quietude in the relaxation pose at the end of a challenging practice.

Step 8. And at last, total enlightenment, the final step of the yoga path, is the **experience of complete wholeness.** This happens when you are in the flow, absorbed in the moment, and feel a connection to all living things. This step, coined *samadhi,* may seem a little new agey, but really it's just another way of saying inner peace, bliss, or freedom.

By observing the eightfold path, the hip tranquil chick is able to blend the practice of yoga into mindful shopping, conscious relationships, and self-awareness. This path helps to transform everyday drama into a source of growth and opportunity. Through breathwork, mindful movement, attention to your thoughts and actions, and finding a tranquil space through meditation, you are able to find a sense of serenity in your everyday. So very apropos!

Hip Tranquil Chick Commandments

The modern girl is faced with numerous decisions on a daily basis—which flavor of lip gloss to purchase, whether to move cross-country to pursue a promising career, how to spend money and time. By implementing the traditional yoga moral codes into everyday living, you are able to use these guideposts as a way to make sure you're living with intention and integrity. These guideposts are not to be confused with rules or dogma; rather, add them to your tranquility tool kit to assist with making decisions and creating an overall healthy lifestyle. The Hip Tranquil Chick Commandments will help you move toward

. . . .

I change myself, I change the world.
—Gloria Anzaldúa

. . . .

a more authentic and commanding destination. Who doesn't want a little nudge, pulse taker, or assurance along this fabulous modern girl journey? Well, look no further than these five-thousand-year-old teachings.

As noted previously, these commandments are broken down into five basic dos and five basic don'ts. Learn to become more and more conscious of how these guide your day-to-day activities, and observe with gratitude how they help channel your practice into living your yoga. Here are fuller definitions of these ten guiding forces, along with ideas on how they play out in your everyday, fast-paced life.

Niyamas: Hip Tranquil Chick Dos

Here are the long-awaited dos—actions or observances that are encouraged of yoginis. Play with the various ways to incorporate them into your lifestyle—while washing dishes, shopping, managing a department of creative nonlinear-thinking girls, having a not-so-easy chat with your beau. Explore turning these into habits.

Purity (*saucha*)—Cleanliness is next to "goddessness." Strive to improve order in your life through conscious consumption and pure intentions, and avoid toxins that could hinder your growth on and off the yoga mat. You appreciate a clean body by filling it with pure, nutritious fuel; create a soulful, serene environment that nourishes your spirit; and develop an innate internal goodness that helps you distinguish right from wrong. By embodying purity, you will be also able to turn mistakes into lessons learned, make amends when necessary, and realize when it is best to let go in order to stay pure to yourself.

Modern girl scenario: Choose herbal tea over espresso, grilled tofu over cheese fries, order over chaos, pure intention over pretense, and compassion over competition.

. . . .

Twenty years from now you will be
more disappointed by the things
you didn't do than by the ones you
did do. So throw off the bowlines.
Sail away from the safe harbor.
—Mark Twain

. . . .

Contentment (*samtosha*)—The hip tranquil chick views challenges as opportunities and cultivates a sense of gratitude for lessons learned. Being content does not equal complacency. It does mean, however, that you savor the present moment and accept situations and people for what they are. By being in the present moment, you will be able to let go of past regrets and future worries by focusing on the here and now. Living in a state of contentment means that you don't lose sight of the big picture, but that you allow yourself to revel in where you are at this moment. This satisfied state ensures freedom from the struggle to keep up with the Joneses.

Modern girl scenario: When bombarded by the media's idea of what clothes, car, or beverage you need to be happy, reflect upon all you have with a sense of gratitude and satisfaction.

Austerity (*tapas*)—Self-discipline and determination is how you move toward your goals. Just as heating an object makes it more malleable, so does discipline allow you to change and grow. This heat (*tapas*) brings transformation and allows the hip tranquil chick to be mindful of making sacrifices in order to move further along on the spiritual path. The effects of consistency in your spiritual practices, such as yoga, meditation, reading, and self-observation, will be evident in your daily routine. The accumulation of unnecessary material possessions will be avoided.

Modern girl scenario: When you are feeling stagnant or stuck in a situation, upping your efforts through discipline and perseverance brings profound results.

Self-study (*svadhyaya*)—The continual introspective study of self and spirituality is prominent on the hip tranquil chick's radar. She explores patterns, relationships, reactions, and even yoga practice habits through regular journal writing and reflection. Through meditation and contemplation, she observes her "monkey mind" in all of its splendor. Through self-study, she is able to rein it all back in to refocus on small changes. She knows that knowledge is power and strives to constantly grow in her many areas of intrigue.

Modern girl scenario: When you notice a recurring pattern in relationships, such as breakdowns in communication or disappointment, review the commonalities, note how your actions or expectations contributed, and take steps to break these patterns.

Surrender to God(dess) (*ishvara pranidhana*)—*Isvara* translates as "Lord" and *pranidhana* as giving up, so this *niyama* is a focus on letting go. Sometimes the best way to handle a challenge is to have faith in a divine plan and surrender control to the way you think things *should* be. Remember, *should* is a bad word! Acknowledge that fighting life only saps energy, and that surrendering comes from a place of strength, rather than weakness. Highs and lows are a part of modern girl life. Observe when it is time to release the ego, cease struggling, and move forward by surrendering to yourself.

Modern girl scenario: Recognize how your efforts on a daily basis contribute to a bigger universal picture, and begin each day by setting an intention and staying mindful of it throughout your day. Pay attention to the opening of one door when another closes.

Yamas: Hip Tranquil Chick Don'ts

The five don'ts in the yogic tradition help guide the modern girl toward happiness and fulfillment. These precepts assist you in taking the high road, living a life filled with dignity, and having the insight to know when a wrong turn has been made. By avoiding these five universal no-nos (violence, lying, stealing, excess, greed), you are sure to help spread tranquility.

. . . .

There are two ways of spreading light: to be the candle, or the mirror that reflects it.
—EDITH WHARTON

. . . .

Nonviolence/Nonharming (*ahimsa*)—This *yama* is interpreted in many ways, ranging from strict vegetarianism to the elimination of negative thoughts or harmful habits toward yourself and others. Apply this precept to help guide your yoga and life practice through observing your thoughts and reactions. Because actions begin with a thought, thinking in a positive, compassionate way about yourself and others is pertinent to spiritual growth. The practice of *ahimsa* must include you. This is where self-care and healthy habits come in.

Modern girl scenario: Become more in tune with yourself and know when to take child's pose rather than one more chaturanga, or to relax in a bubble bath instead of saying yes to another cocktail party invite.

Truthfulness (*satya*)—Using words, thoughts, and actions mindfully is important to the hip tranquil chick. Value being honest with yourself and others. Avoid putting yourself in situations that would cause you to deviate from your truth. When you realize that you've said yes and wanted to say no, make amends to honor your choices in the future. Believe in being true to your values, honoring your boundaries, and living with integrity.

Modern girl scenario: If your idea of a perfect Saturday night is drinking sparkling apple cider while draped over your chaise lounge in your cashmere pajamas, then say "No, thanks" to a late night of dancing with the girls.

Nonstealing (*asteya*)—The hip tranquil chick would never shoplift from Sephora, nor would she take her colleague's idea as her own. Constantly develop your own sense of self and creativity while honoring your teachers along the way. Do not steal from yourself by misusing your time or resources through participation in activities that don't guide you toward your dreams. *Asteya* goes well beyond taking someone else's possessions, and extends into subtleties of stealing that may prevent you from fulfilling your potential.

Modern girl scenario: Staying in a job that you know is a dead end when you dream of launching an online baby boutique is a form of stealing from yourself. You are stealing your own chances for success by playing it safe. Take action to make changes that reward your time and efforts so that you are giving to yourself and others. Make it a win-win.

Moderation (*brahmacharya*)—Even though the hip tranquil chick has a devout love of passion and a desire for succulence, she knows when enough is enough. Avoid overindulgence, recognize that all good things can become a crutch, and constantly seek the middle path. When practicing yoga, both on and off the mat, seek balance, simple indulgences, and surrender the "addiction" when a problem is detected.

Modern girl scenario: Seek moderation by indulging in small doses, especially in sensual cravings such as chocolate mousse, soy chai lattes, sex, shopping, and yoga.

Tranquil Tip: When you find yourself glum because you didn't practice *brahmacharya* and you have a horrible hangover from one too many cosmos or a bellyache from too many pieces of Godiva chocolate, do the following: (1) acknowledge your mistakes, (2) learn your lesson, (3) embrace self-compassion (you can't *always* be perfect), (4) grab your silk eye pillow, a huge glass of sparkling water, and make your way into legs-up-the-wall pose.

Greedlessness (*aparigraha*)—Do not covet another's yoga practice, perceived spiritual wisdom, material possessions, or life. Instead of wishing you had this handbag or possessed that *je ne sais quoi*, be happy with what you have, rejoice in the good fortune of others, and never waste precious time with jealousy. Seek to simplify rather than accumulate. Graciously give of yourself and your resources. Let compliments and gratitude toward others flow plentifully.

Modern girl scenario: Recognize when shopping, the perfection of yoga poses, and acquiring material goods exceed a healthy dose of retail therapy or spirituality and become an unquenchable desire for more. Work to remove such patterns and continue on a simple, yet abundant path free of longing.

Help sprinkle doses of tranquility into other people's lives through simple gestures such as giving the car in the next lane ample space to merge into yours, allowing the fashionista with one head of organic lettuce to move ahead of you in the long line, directing the exhausted tourist back to her hotel, or making space for the frazzled latecomer in yoga class. These small efforts pay off in the long run and earn you bonus karma points along the way.

Tranquil Tip: Thoughts are the seeds that blossom into action. Live well by doing good to those whom you come across each day. Remember, if you do good things, good things will happen to you. The law of karma holds this promise. Come on, girls, hold your head high, wear a vibrant smile, and let your presence have a positive effect on everyone you meet. Be a do-gooding diva gone wild.

Modern Girl Mojo

Through the law of karma, every action has an equal and opposite reaction. By allowing these guideposts to direct you during everyday drama, you make more conscious decisions and receive credit into your karma bank account. Musings on the moral precepts of yoga help us to see how these ancient teachings relate to our modern-day trials and tribulations (also known as "growth opportunities"). By using the Hip Tranquil Chick Commandments, we move closer to a flow-filled lifestyle. Imagine a life filled with contentment, reflection, and compassion toward yourself and others. By adhering to these tenets and taking your yoga beyond physical poses, you will find tranquility naturally.

. . . .

How people treat you is their karma; how you react is yours.
—WAYNE DYER

. . . .

Omwork

Take one week (or month) to focus on each of the eight steps of yoga. Choose one and stay mindful of how the practice of that step affects your choices, observations, impressions, and actions. Write about your experience with a detailed description of what that particular facet of yoga looks and feels like to you after a week or month of deep connection to it.

Ponder how the dos and don'ts can assist your growth in life, both on and off the yoga mat. For example, practicing *ahimsa* allows me to take a restorative practice over an advanced practice when I'm feeling exhausted, and it also encourages me to choose kind words over harsh ones when handling a delicate situation.

Explore the Hip Tranquil Chick Commandments. Dive into each of the 10 do's and don'ts over the next 10 months. As you make decisions, explore options, and observe patterns, reflect on how you can live this individual moral code with more habitual grace and ease.

Savvy Sources

Read

Yoga and the Path of the Urban Mystic, by Darren Main

Living Your Yoga: Finding the Spiritual in Everyday Life, by Judith Lasater

The Wisdom of No Escape: And the Path of Loving Kindness, by Pema Chodron

Yoga Body, Buddha Mind, by Cyndi Lee

Meditations from the Mat: Daily Reflections on the Path of Yoga, by Rolf Gates and Katrina Kenison

Happy Yoga: 7 Reasons Why There's Nothing to Worry About, by Steve Ross

Girl Seeks Bliss: Zen and the Art of Modern Life Maintenance, by Nicole Beland

Yoga Journal magazine

Shambhala Sun magazine

Visit

www.dailyzen.com

www.dailyom.com

Listen

Breath of the Heart, by Krishna Das

The Lover and the Beloved, by Donna De Lory

Now, by Bhagavan Das

Embrace, by Deva Premal

Temple of Love, by Rasa

When you inhale, you are taking

the strength from God.

When you exhale, it represents the

service you are giving to the world.

—B. K. S. IYENGAR

Part II

Yoga off the Mat

Yoga off the mat is where the
benefits of your practice connect
with your core.

Inner Chic

The inner chic portion of the hip tranquil chick journey is the process of exploring yoga further by tuning in to your vision, self-care, and deep connection to creativity.

Chapter 4

Visionary Value

infuse your life with a value-led vision

· ·

Your intent should pour out of you. It should emanate from

every cell of your being so that you attract the people and

circumstances that can support you in manifesting your desires.

—DIANNE COLLINS

A mindful maven jump-starts hip tranquil chickness by reflecting on how she will serve the world and creating a vision statement for her life. Explore what you want out of life, how you'll leave a legacy, and how your mark on this world will be meaningful. It is true that the unexamined life is not worth living, and if there is not a clearly defined direction, the path toward your dream life may be very winding. Grounded in intention, take the time to determine your values, goals, and overall vision to help you grow into a successful and savvy hip tranquil chick.

Intention

Intention is a fancy way of saying "a purpose or plan." At the beginning of every yoga class at Tranquil Space, we encourage students to set an intention for their practice. We suggest internal questions such as, Why am I on the yoga mat? What am I hoping to gain or shed through my practice? What is going on mentally, physically, and emotionally for me at this time? How can I capture this with a clear intention?

· ·

Our intention creates our reality.
—WAYNE DYER

· ·

By creating mindful intentions, we are able to get clear on why we're doing what we do. For example, when we began offering trunk shows at the studio, they were touted as "retail therapy" events. This was confusing to some yogis. Why is a yoga studio promoting shopping nights? When I became clearer on my intention behind the trunk shows, I was able to create the tagline "empowering women to create," find the perfect charity to share proceeds with (the Fund for Women Artists), and explain succinctly how the trunk shows aligned perfectly with the studio's vision to support and nurture women to grow creatively.

 Tranquil Tip: Ponder your off-the-mat intentions. When you wake up in the morning, what is your intention for the day? Do you want to do two random acts of kindness or be a calming influence for the chaos around you? When you show up in the boardroom, what is your intention for the meeting? When you greet your family or friends after a long day, what is your intention for that initial interaction that may set the tone for the rest of the evening?

Explore how getting clear on intentions can help you determine your vision. Maybe you're holding out on happiness until you find the perfect partner. But upon further reflection, you realize that what you're really wanting is a more active social life that includes oodles of dates and girls' nights out. Maybe you're practicing yoga to lose weight and get fit. But then you realize that you're developing a deeper spiritual connection, which has become your focus with yoga, while getting toned is an added benefit.

> You must do the thing which
> you think you cannot do.
> —ELEANOR ROOSEVELT

Wave Goodbye to "If Only"

Life can become a series of "if onlys" and "should haves" if we don't take time to confront our fears, set intentions, and take action. When I began college, I recall hearing from a wise senior sorority sister that you regret the things you don't do more than the things that you do. This encouraged me to be okay with making mistakes, pushing my edges, and taking chances. Our fears, however, can be very powerful and keep us from attaining or even exploring our vision.

 Tranquil Tip: Take a moment to identify a few of your "if onlys." If only I had more money, more confidence, less fear, more time, less weight, different clothes, a better boss, a better family, a nicer partner, or a partner at all. Do any of these resonate? Time and money seem to be the big "if onlys" for most hip chicks. Ponder what you would do if time and money weren't an issue. Would you write a screenplay, live on a houseboat in Paris, serve in the Peace Corps in Uganda, move to Hollywood to pursue acting? Disregarding the obstacles of time and money opens up amazing possibilities that may surprise you.

Play with switching your scarcity mentality to one of abundance. There is plenty of abundance to go around. Operate under the assumption that you have everything you need to begin living the life of your dreams. Bringing it all together will take a shuffling of priorities and time with lots of discipline (*tapas*) and, most of all, patience, but the reward of tranquility and contentment will be worth it.

Identify and Exemplify Your Values

A value is a principle or standard that you hold dear, a quality that you admire, seek to emulate, and strive for on a regular basis. Here is a selection of values that may be important to you. Run through the list and circle those that jump out at you. Don't think too much, trust your gut, and choose those that resonate with your polished personality.

accomplishment
adventure
affection
arts
beauty
challenge
communication
community
creativity
discipline
discovery

education
efficiency
environmentalism
faith
fame
flair
freedom
fun
global view
gratitude
hard work

honesty
independence
innovation
inspiration
integrity
leadership
love
loyalty
meaning
peace
personal growth
pleasure
power
problem solving

prosperity
recognition
relationships
reputation
service
simplicity
sophistication
strength
tradition
tranquility
trust
truth
wealth
wisdom

· · · · · · · · · · · · · · · · · · · ·

The important thing is this: to be able at any moment to sacrifice what we are for what we could become.
—CHARLES DuBois

The Value of a Vision Statement

By taking the time to reflect and set intentions, you'll be able to determine your vision, notice what moves you, what ignites passion, and what you admire in others. It can be as specific as opening a much-needed natural health food store in your neighborhood, or as global and grandiose as changing the world through activist efforts. A vision statement is what you want to create for your life: what you want to become, and why it is important to you.

You may dream of creating a retreat center in Costa Rica, designing couture children's clothing, writing a sassy chick lit series, or starting a family and living on the beach. Identify your skill set—organizing, following through, taking initiative, listening, singing, drawing. Ponder what you are doing when you lose track of time. Explore ways to incorporate more of these activities into your life.

If you long to excel in public speaking, leadership, painting, or financial analysis but are still at the starting line, delve into these skills. By taking stock of your dreams, strengths, and weaknesses, you'll be better able to craft the ultimate vision for your life.

By clarifying your values, you will be able to understand your feelings and needs, along with what makes you tick overall. Choose your top five values from the boxed section and highlight them. See if you can incorporate their meaning into your vision. I chose

. . . .

I have the same goal I've had since I was a little girl. I want to rule the world.

—MADONNA

. . . .

flair, independence, innovation, leadership, and tranquility as my top five values. My vision statement is: I seek to live life fully and flairfully, and to inspire others to do the same, while enjoying tranquility and independence along the way. This connects my values and helps me guide my leadership and innovation toward a consistent theme—helping others and myself grow in a deep and playful way.

Unveil Your Vision

It may seem odd to focus on figuring out what you like. You may be very in touch with what you prefer. But sometimes we can get stuck in a place where we feel as if we've lost

. . . .

When you determine what you want, you have made the most important decision in your life.

—DOUGLAS LURTAN

. . . .

a connection to our innermost self. For example, after being in a loveless partnership, a passionless career, or running on a treadmill for years, it can be hard to connect to these authentic and deeply personal places. Let's dig deeper together.

 Tranquil Tip: If you come across a mental block when attempting to tap into your vision, you might benefit from opening your body up first through a yoga session, a run, dancing around your apartment, or a hike through nature.

Brainstorm. To help you reconnect to these passion-filled roots, which I promise are there but may need some gentle unearthing, indulge in some quiet time. Grab a journal, head to the neighborhood café, and devote an hour to exploring what's in your heart.

1. Write 20 passions that bring you pure bliss: running races, writing poetry, listening to live jazz.
2. Write 10 causes that inspire you: stopping global warming, animal rights, mentoring, registering young women to vote.
3. Write out your top 10 strengths: meeting deadlines, telling stories, strategic thinking, decorating, event planning.

Do you see a common theme among these three lists? Are you observing that you're a mover and shaker who is also crazy about crocheting? Did your inner politico rear its head after many years of being subdued? Is there a pull toward more playfulness in your corporate culture? Spend time reflecting on these synchronicities. Brainstorm on ways to tie together seemingly unrelated preferences, passions, and strengths.

Visualize. Visualization is a way for you to imagine what you want to manifest. Picture yourself living your most fabulously hip and tranquil life.

1. When you get up in the morning, what time is it? Do you rise with the sun or sleep until noon?
2. Do you live in the city, near the beach, in the mountains, or in the suburbs?
3. How do you dress for the day: power suit or T-shirt and sandals?
4. Do you go into an office or work at home?
5. What does your home look like: surrounded by flowers in a country cottage or a minimalist city loft?
6. Who do you share it with: a goldfish, partner, large family, or good girlfriends?
7. What is your typical day like?
8. What do you eat: gourmet meals you spend hours preparing, or dinner out at the latest swanky hot spot?
9. When you get home, how do you spend the evening: with a good book, writing, in night classes learning a new trade, or straight to bed due to exhilarating workdays?
10. How do you care for yourself during the day: lunchtime stroll or express yoga class midday?

Bring to mind a clear image of what you want to create, combined with a strong positive emotion. For example, if your desire is to have a relationship and move to San Francisco, you may envision yourself in the arms of a beloved while strolling through Golden Gate Park. Or if you want to design a dress, visualize yourself showing the finished product at a local shopping event featuring emerging

> Imagination is everything. It is the preview of life's coming attractions.
> —ALBERT EINSTEIN.

designers. Or if a much-needed vacation is a hope over the summer, visualize yourself in a teeny polka dot bikini, lying poolside with an umbrella drink and a saucy novel. The ideas are limitless, so play with this and capture your vision with images through collage making, drawing, or writing it out as a story.

Repeat an Affirmation. An affirmation is a clear, concise, positive statement in the present tense claiming that what you want is happening. For example, if you're hoping to start the new year with a fresh fitness regime, you could use "I am toned, healthy, and feel comfortable in my own skin." If you're hoping to increase your social network with successful friends, try "I am surrounded by inspiring people who encourage me to move forward." If you want your business to grow, repeat "My business is thriving and I share my abundance with those who work with me and the clients I serve through my work." Be creative. There is no right or wrong affirmation.

 Tranquil Tip: It is important to continue repeating the affirmation until it feels like it is part of you. Post it where you'll see it on a regular basis—your bathroom mirror, car dashboard, or refrigerator. Let it serve as a way to bring you out of those disenchanted moments we all experience from time to time.

Create a Vision Statement

A vision statement is a simple promise to the world that your presence on this earth is not in vain, but grounded in true intention. Review your values, interests, and passions. Remember, be clear on what you want and why you want it. More than likely the "why" has to do with your values. For example, you may want to direct a theatrical production, design a clothing line, write a book, or start a movement. These ideas could be motivated by gaining recognition, serving others, shedding light on a controversial issue, or solving a need. Take a moment to answer this question, What is the legacy I want to leave? Let this be the question that helps you create your vision statement.

Sample vision statements: I want to live abundantly by creating a business that inspires women to look and feel their best. I want to create a hip tranquil chick movement that helps women live life fully and boldly. I want to nurture a loving, happy family. I want to live abundantly and exploit my creative side by designing clothing for canines and writing canine care books.

 Tranquil Tip: If writing out a linear vision statement doesn't work for you, there are a few ways to play with your visionary concept creatively to determine your vision statement. **Create a collage** with images that appeal to your future self. Determine their commonalities. **Make a list** of the things you know you want in life. Narrow down the list into one concise statement. **Paint or draw** your ideal vision. What does it look like to you? How can you translate the image into a statement? Mind map your vision by starting with key words or images that speak to you and watch a masterpiece unfold by connecting concepts to your overall ideal.

> The most pathetic person in the world is someone who has sight, but no vision.
> —HELEN KELLER

Explore the power of getting your vision down on paper. Read your vision statement every day. Keep it in mind when planning your daily activities. Have it boldly and colorfully written in your planner or Palm. Take one stepping-stone each day in the direction of your vision.

Get Your Goals On

Living your vision out loud takes more than simply creating your inspiring vision statement. Now is your chance to determine the stepping-stones that will get you closer to your vision. Do this by setting TRANQUIL goals and creating action steps that relate to the goals. TRANQUIL stands for time bound, reasonable, action focused, niche filling, quenching a passion, uniform with values, intention driven, and lovable. When creating goals, ask yourself the following questions to help ensure all components of the goal are intact and aligned with your passions.

> If you're bored with life—you don't get up every morning with a burning desire to do things—you don't have enough goals.
> —LOU HOLTZ

- Does your goal have a timeline: by the end of this month, quarter, or year?
- Is your goal reasonable? Are you setting yourself up for strategic success?
- Is your goal action focused? Determine the steps associated with your dream.
- Is your goal a niche made especially for you? Keep your goals as unique as your personality.
- Does your goal quench a passion that you hold dear? If not, let it go.
- Does your goal align with your values? Is this goal a piece of your ideal vision?
- Do you have a strong intention to carry out your goal? Make sure you're highly motivated to make it happen.
- Is your goal lovable? Are you crazy about what you're wanting to do? If not, scratch it, rewrite it, or let it go altogether!

Tranquil Tip: Ponder 10 goals, either one-year or five-year. One-year goals may include getting certified to teach vinyasa yoga, completing a business plan, or writing a book proposal. A five-year goal may be opening a yoga studio, getting published in *O*, or becoming a well-known speaker on feminist issues with at least 25 paid speaking engagements per year.

Weave common themes together to create a vision statement for your life, then write an affirmation to support this goal.

Put Your Vision Statement into Play

Be mindful of your vision and allow it to change as you grow. Keep the big picture in mind when making decisions and take action each and every day. By developing a connection to your vision, you are able to align your world with your values to stay on your stylish, strong, and well-intentioned path. Use the Hip Tranquil Chick Commandments as guideposts to help stay on track.

> One's philosophy is not best expressed in words; it is expressed in the choices one makes.
> —ELEANOR ROOSEVELT

Don't panic if you face a setback, change of heart, or small derailment. We've all heard that when one door closes, another opens. Use that concept to help pick yourself up, dust off, and hit the ground running again. Winding roads sometimes make for a very fun and lesson-filled journey.

Apply the TRANQUIL concept to your dreams. Break them down into concrete steppingstones. Review your vision statement and goals regularly. Take action daily in the direction of your vision. No more "if onlys." It's all about making things happen. Watch your vision unfold one stiletto step at a time.

Omwork

Post your vision statement in places that are visible to you during your everyday routine: in your planner, on the back of your cell phone, on your car visor, inside the kitchen cabinet that holds your morning teacups, on your bathroom mirror, framed on your desk. This way you are constantly reminded of why you're here and where you're going.

Review your vision statement seasonally to ensure it still resonates for you. Reflect. Make necessary changes. Revamp the statement to correspond with new directions you may be taking. Let the evolutionary process be as powerful as the creation of your visionary concept.

Set TRANQUIL goals seasonally. Divide your goals up into the various hats that you wear: mother, student, teacher, sister, friend, designer, writer, employee, employer, manager, visionary, merchandiser, buyer, partner, and so on. Or divide your goals up into the various pieces of your life—health, finances, relationships, career, creativity, spirituality, home environment, and self-care. Write your goals for the hats you wear or your life categories on colorful index cards. Hang them above your desk as a constant reminder.

Savvy Sources

Read

The Purpose of Your Life: Finding Your Place in the World Using Synchronicity, Intuition, and Uncommon Sense, by Carol Adrienne and James Redfield

The Success Principles: How to Get from Where You Are to Where You Want to Be, by Jack Canfield

The Best Year of Your Life: Dream It, Plan It, Live It, by Debbie Ford

Clarity Quest: How to Take a Sabbatical Without Taking More Than a Week Off, by Pamela Ammondson

Live Your Best Life: A Treasury of Wisdom, Wit, Advice, Interviews, and Inspiration from O, the Oprah Magazine, by O, the Oprah Magazine

Visioning: Ten Steps to Designing the Life of Your Dreams, by Lucia Capacchione

Creative Visualization: Use the Power of Your Imagination to Create What You Want in Your Life, by Shakti Gawain

The Alchemist: A Fable about Following Your Dream, by Paulo Coelho

Oh, the Places You'll Go, by Dr. Seuss

Visit

www2.oprah.com

Listen

Melelana, by Keali'i Reichel

Hey You!, by Youssou N'Dour

Faith, by George Michael

Euro Lounge, by various artists

Garden State soundtrack, by various artists

Chapter 5

Self-Nurturing Survival

discover the art of being selfish

· ·

Eternally, woman spills herself away in driblets to

the thirsty, seldom being allowed the time, the quiet,

the peace, to let the pitcher fill up to the brim.

—Anne Morrow Lindbergh

Yoga is all about connecting the body, mind, and soul. When we neglect or abuse any aspect of this balance, we can lose touch with who we are at the core. Through our yoga practice, we are more likely to reflect and be conscious of the warning signs when this connection is unbalanced. With a commitment to self-care, we can relish in energy, creativity, and best of all . . . tranquility.

The hip tranquil chick shines best when her internal well is full from self-replenishing. As the flight attendant instructs you before the airplane takes off, put on your own life mask before assisting another. In order to be fully fabulous, you must be filled with fuel, not running on E with the red light flashing. Even as an active, vivacious yoga lover, you can get caught on life's treadmill with the

best of them—spending 12-hour days at the office, running from event to event, skipping yoga and meals. Realize when it is time to leap off, reassess, and spend some downtime recharging. Then you can, once again, present your most sophisticated (and sane) self to the world.

· ·

To keep the body in good health is a duty . . . otherwise we shall not be able to keep our mind strong and clear.
—Buddha

· ·

Body

Your body is one of your best teachers, and by learning to listen to its messages, you will find yourself making healthier and more holistic decisions. Begin to treat your body

Yummy Yin Yoga

In yin yoga you hold poses for at least several minutes while stretching the connective tissue around a joint. Forget alignment, let go of expectations, breathe deeply, and savor this yummy self-care yoga practice. Try the following of my fave yin poses:

1. **Dragon pose:** Begin in table pose. Place your left foot between your hands. Wiggle your right knee back until you feel an opening in the hips. Place your hands on your left knee. Breathe here for 1 to 5 minutes. Repeat on the other side.

2. **Seal pose:** Begin on your belly and extend your arms out diagonally from the shoulders to a raised 45-degree angle, with your hands on the floor. Let your shoulders move up comfortably toward the ears, soften the spine, and support your weight on your arms. Breathe here for 1 to 5 minutes.

3. **Seated forward bend:** Extend your legs out in front of your hips. Walk your hands toward your feet, lower your head, relax your legs, and let your spine round. Breathe here for 3 to 5 minutes.

4. **Cross-legged reclining spinal twist:** Lie on your back and hug your knees into your chest. Cross your right leg over your left. Lower your legs to the floor. Extend your arms straight out to the sides. Lower your right shoulder to the floor. Breathe here for 1 to 2 minutes. Repeat on the other side.

with special care and notice when any of the following creeps into your life: a lack of sleep, an unhealthy diet, tension, a lack of energy, a neglected yoga practice. To truly practice self-care, it is imperative that you treat your body as a sacred temple.

6 Swanky Spinal Movements

Ensure that the six movements of the spine each day are coupled with lighthearted movement and, of course, laughter. You will be able to open up the parts of your body that are feeling constricted due to stress, anxiety, or exhaustion. This will allow for more flow in your life.

Begin in a comfortable seated pose on the floor with your spine long and your shoulders over your hips. Place your hands on your knees. Find your breath.

1. **Back bend:** Inhale, lift your heart center, draw your shoulder blades in and down, and arch the upper back.

2. **Forward bend:** Exhale, draw your navel toward your spine, drop your chin to your chest, and curve the spine forward.

3. **Right side bend:** Inhale, return to a neutral spine with shoulders over hips,

and extend your arms along your ears. Exhale, lower your right hand to the floor near your right hip, and extend the left arm alongside your left ear.

4. **Left side bend:** Inhale, return to a neutral spine with shoulders over hips, and extend your arms along your ears. Exhale, lower your left hand to the floor near your left hip, and extend your right arm alongside your right ear.

5. **Twist to right:** Inhale, return to a neutral spine with shoulders over hips, and extend your arms up alongside your ears. Exhale, place your left hand on your right knee, and cartwheel your right arm behind you. Let your gaze follow.

6. **Twist to left:** Inhale, return to a neutral spine with shoulders over hips, and extend your arms alongside your ears. Exhale, place your right hand on your left knee, and cartwheel your left arm behind you. Let your gaze follow. Inhale, return to a neutral spine, and repeat this sequence 4 more times.

Know Your Body

Observe your body's special requests. Whether you live on salted almonds and kale or fast-food burgers and french fries, the key is to listen to your body's reactions and cravings. You may find yourself wanting to call it an early night when everyone else is out buzzing about town. Your body is constantly sending you messages on its needs, desires, and discomforts. Tapping into this subtle communication is a big benefit of your yoga practice and beyond.

Inner Clarity

Have you gotten a headache right before a big soirée you've been dreading or experienced that sinking feeling in your belly when you have to handle a not-so-pleasant situation? Do you avoid phone calls or plans with certain friends or family members because you know you're going to be ruffled afterwards? We've all experienced these subtle messages from our body. Intuition can show

Nourishing Treats for the Girl-on-the-Go

As a busy girl expending tons of energy through yoga on and off the mat, you need to nourish your insides. • Surround yourself with fresh fruit and vegetables. You can also use them to decorate! I always have a vibrant bowl of lemons in my home to help inspire a state of cheer. • Master the art of salad making—toss together greens, grapes, tomatoes, almonds for crunch, blueberries for color, slices of avocado, goat or feta cheese, and Newman's oil and vinegar dressing. Yum! • Cook with whole grains such as brown rice, steel-cut oats, and millet. • Be sure to always have a handful of tamari-roasted almonds or roasted pumpkin seeds nearby as a midday pick-me-up. • Never leave home without your water bottle filled to the brim garnished with a sliver of lemon, lime, or cucumber. A hip tranquil chick must stay hydrated. • Invest in an impressive array of teas and drink a cup of decaffeinated green doused with honey or agave nectar daily.

up as feelings or insights and often arise when you're in a relaxed state—practicing in yoga class, taking a hot bath, walking through the woods. By paying attention to how you're feeling after spending time with people or after certain situations, you're better able to connect to your body. This ensures you make decisions to devote time to replenishing versus depleting ways.

. . . .

Supporting others without nurturing ourselves depletes energy necessary for developing creativity.
—C. Diane Ealy

. . . .

 Tranquil Tip: If you're having trouble connecting to your intuitive side, chances are you need to slow down in order to hear your inner voice. Carve out some alone time and pull out your yoga mat, sit on a meditation cushion, or simply hop into the bathtub. Then visualize your mind empty of all thoughts. Allow your body to relax completely. Ask a question or visualize the situation or person in question, and observe what sensations or thoughts arise. You may be able to get an answer based on how your body reacts to the question. If not, be patient and watch for synchronistic events that unfold over the next few days. Repeat this process often and feel yourself connecting deeper to your authentic, intuitive side.

Mind Your Mind

Taking good care of your mind reaps numerous rewards, both personally and professionally. When you find yourself giving too much of your time, money, or talents, lacking clarity about personal goals, feeling forgetful or absentminded, or focusing critically on the past or future, it is time to reconnect with some apropos mental self-care. Explore the ideas in "Time Is Precious" for rekindling this internal connection.

. . . .

Most folks are about as happy as they make up their minds to be.
—Abraham Lincoln

Time Is Precious

Juggling a busy schedule with grace is how the hip tranquil chick keeps it together. The first step is to handle your biggest, most important tasks first rather than knocking minor to-dos off the list and leaving little time for what matters most. Always ask, "What is the most valuable use of my time right now?" Determine your priorities and take steps daily to accomplish them. Among other things, the 80/20 rule means that most people achieve 80 percent of their goals through 20 percent of their efforts. This rule serves as a reminder to focus more of your time and energy on the 20 percent of your work that offers the biggest return. Prioritize, connect to your TRANQUIL goals, avoid time zappers (pointless meetings, chatty phone calls, constant checking of e-mail), delegate, and get an organizing system that works well for you (electronic Palm, old-school planner pad). Getting a grasp on time management is sure to bring you tranquility.

Spin the Wheel

For many of us, life balance seems like an unattainable feat. However, by regularly reflecting on how you're doing overall, you can bring your life into a more balanced state.

During hip tranquil chick workshops and retreats, we do an exercise called the wheel of life, where we rate eight main areas of our life: health, finances, relationships, career, creativity, spirituality, home environment, and self-care. Pull out your journal or a colorful sheet of paper and draw a circle with eight spokes labeled with the main life categories listed above. Then draw a line through each spoke indicating how satisfied you are with that category. A ranking of 0 will be at the center and means not at all satisfied, and 10 will be at the edge and means sensationally satisfied.

This simple exercise can open your eyes to how delighted you are in any given area. You can see concretely how balanced (or unbalanced) your life wheel is at any time. Observe your three lowest-ranked categories and choose three basic steps you can begin taking immediately to improve your satisfaction in that area. For example, if self-care is low, schedule one hour to write in your journal or make a pedi appointment. If creativity is low, visit your local art store and get inspired to draw, paint, scrapbook, or knit.

Tranquil Tip: You have 168 hours each week to fill. For a hip tranquil chick, that is easily done. However, it's helpful to reflect on how it is broken down. Hopefully you're sleeping for at least 42 of these hours, but what about the remaining 122? Spend a week tracking your time, and you may be surprised how many hours are taken up with "time suckers" such as surfing the Internet, watching TV, chatting on trivial phone calls, being with draining friends, and attending events that no longer sustain you. Observe where you can make some changes. Find some open space to take better care of yourself and your passions.

Life can get out of whack when too much time is spent on any particular category that leaves little room for play in the others. For example, a heavy imbalance occurs if tons of time is spent in the social life and relationships category, and little time is spent in career or finances. If you're out with your paramour smooching into the wee hours nightly, you will not have the juice to be fully present when handed a new, stimulating project at the office. Observe where there is imbalance to help establish a plan for moving toward a more cohesive and fulfilling lifestyle. Reflect on what energizes and what drains you. Then make some conscious changes.

Journal Writing Tips and Tricks

I've been an avid journal writer since grade school. Sure, my early entries consisted of who was my new BFF that day, what I ate for lunch, and who was my new "love." But, thank goodness, with time they have evolved into more substantive material. I find this process to be a therapeutic brain dump, and believe it has saved me lots of time, regrets, and money in therapy bills.

Journal writing can serve as a light into your dark, unexplored places. Here are some tips for using your journal as inexpensive and convenient bedside therapy:

1. **How to write?** I prefer a compact spiral-bound hardcover journal for easy transport. Using colored pens, scented colored pencils, highlighters, or an average blue ballpoint works for me. You may prefer loose-leaf paper or a large art book and calligraphy pens. Either way, make sure your journal reflects who you are and works for your lifestyle.

Jump-Start Your Journaling

Don't worry about punctuation or grammar. Let your pen dance freely across the page. You can doodle, paint, make lists, mind map, ask questions, relive a past experience, fantasize about a future experience, interpret dreams, explore options, jetset, or craft a cathartic letter you don't plan on sending. Remember, there is no right or wrong way to journal.

When stuck, try answering the following to get you going:

- How am I feeling?
- What do I really want?
- Am I happy with my current lifestyle?
- In what ways do I want to grow?
- What are five lessons I have learned recently?
- Am I living in alignment with my vision statement?
- In what ways am I challenging myself?
- How would I describe my overall mood?
- Where can I add more creativity in my life?
- How can I serve?
- Am I noticing patterns that I'd like to change?

Take the time to nurture your relationship with your journal. Ultimately, it will draw you closer to a more insightful relationship with yourself and others. By exploring patterns, reading your repeated scenarios, and observing your fears, you will have a more compassionate and enlightened view of who you are. Journaling is the perfect way to diffuse emotion and help you return to a state of tranquility.

2. **Where to write?** Find a cozy place that allows you to let go. I love to journal in solitude while in bed, at the dog park while Louis runs free, in a quiet café, or in a candlelit bathtub. You may prefer an active Internet café, a bustling local diner, or the hoppin' corner bookstore. The key is to find a place where you can write in comfort without being interrupted.

3. **When to write?** Julia Cameron, the author of *The Artist's Way*, encourages us to write three pages longhand first thing in the morning, before our conscious mind creeps into the writing. Others claim that evening is best, when you're unwinding and wrapping up the day. I believe that you should write when you can squeeze in the time—while riding the metro, waiting at the airport, after putting the kids to bed. Find what works best for your lifestyle and let the thoughts flow. The point is not to add this process to your to-do list, but to make space in your routine with ease.

> In the diary I can keep track
> of the two faces of reality.
> —ANAÏS NIN

4. **What to write?** Ah, now this is the million-dollar question. Staring at a blank page is scary for many of us. Take the plunge! You'll probably be pleasantly surprised with the process. Some days I feel I could write for hours, as I have so many emotions that I need to share in a safe place. Other days, there is very little

motivation for getting past the date and time. In "Jump-Start Your Journaling" I've outlined some of my favorite ways to rock the writing when I encounter an uncomfortable inner silence.

Soul Care

Your soul longs to be nurtured. In our busy lives, this piece of our self-care is easy to forget because it may not scream out in angst quite like the body or mind. However, the soul is important to nurture if you want to live a truly hip and tranquil life. Watch for these warning signs that your soul is askew: acting compulsively; feeling depressed, angry, frustrated, discontented, or alienated from others. If you're experiencing any of these signs, don't wait a minute longer to practice some of the suggested soul soothers.

> The soul is placed in the
> body like a rough diamond,
> and must be polished.
> —DANIEL DEFOE

Soul Restorers

Practice self-compassion. • Observe your self-talk and replace negative comments with positive affirmations. • Say no without guilt. • Indulge yourself occasionally. • Reward your efforts. • Take time off—you deserve it. • Escape the city. • Reconnect with nature. • Let go. • Nibble dark chocolate. • Breathe deeply. • Roll out your yoga mat. • Garden. • Bake bread. • Nap.

Simple Ways to Soothe the Soul

As the Wilde quote at right signifies, the relationship you have with yourself (how you feel about and treat yourself) is significant. Actually, this is the only relationship in life that is 100 percent guaranteed. You are sure to awaken and slumber with yourself each and every day. We all know the importance of taking care of ourselves, but how can this love story become a celebrated regular romance? By taking time to soothe your soul, of course.

Indulge in a weekly solo excursion. Since hip tranquil chicks are always on the go, spending time alone allows for simple reflection and rejuvenation. Taking such sacred time alone each week can help you reconnect with parts of yourself that are often forgotten in the various roles you hold. • Explore a museum and sketch out your favorite painting. • Visit a local winery and sip sauvignon blanc on the veranda while overlooking the vineyard. • Browse through a bookstore to absorb the infinite knowledge surrounding you. • Scope out a new sidewalk café for sipping soy chai latte and watching the passersby. • Book a ticket to an exotic locale where you won't know a soul. • Go to a matinee or theatre production.

Host a solo girl's night in. Nothing recharges your batteries quite like celebrating solo time with all the necessities. Put on your most comfy togs. Pull your hair back, add a headband, and cover your face with a moisturizing mud mask. Gather your journal, girly movies (*Breakfast at Tiffany's, Thelma and Louise, Girls Just Want to Have Fun, Flashdance, Love Actually*), a supply of your numerous to-be-read magazines, bubbly beverages, and favorite foods (pizza, Chinese takeout, dill chips with French onion dip, chocolate cupcakes). Play your favorite big-band tunes and dance around your apartment. Give yourself a foot massage using a peppermint lotion that leaves your feet tingly. Then cover them with fluffy chenille socks. Melt into your chaise longue and let this be a sacred solo night to remember.

. . . .

To love yourself is the beginning
of a lifelong romance.
—Oscar Wilde

. . . .

Home Spa Tips

Self-nurture alone at home with some of these simple ideas:

1. Add 10 bags of chamomile and green tea to your bath. Ahhh!
2. Make a hydrating facial mask by mashing half a banana and a tablespoon each of honey and milk. Leave on your skin for 15 minutes, then rinse off.
3. Add a quart of milk, a pint of cream, and 2 teaspoons of honey to your bath for a moisturizing and luxurious bathing delight.
4. Add 5 drops of essential oil of lavender and rose to your bath.
5. Add rosewater to a small atomizer and mist your hair, clothing, face, and linens. Perfect for enhancing your postpractice glow.

Meditate. Take the time to empty your mind of all the drama. My first mini (day and a half) meditation training was a few years ago in a nearby city, and it left me in distress. On the drive home I called everyone I knew to try to reconnect, even though I had barely been away. I have a love-hate relationship with meditation: being alone with thoughts can be scary, but the results are profound. There are numerous books devoted to this tool, and I'm only touching on the topic, so I encourage you to explore it deeper after starting with the basics here.

Get moving! Of course, the hip tranquil chick gets her yoga on consistently. But since you know how good it makes you feel, how about adding a bit more movement to your everyday routine? • Get off the metro one stop earlier and walk the rest of the way to work. • Take a morning stroll through your neighborhood while the streets are still quiet. • Start your day with a few sun salutes. • Do laps at your local pool or jump in the ocean. • Walk your dog down a new path. • Indulge in a hip-hop, salsa, or tango class. • Jump rope. • Do a cartwheel in the grocery aisle. • Don some snowshoes and do a full moon trek.

Move in ways you never thought possible and observe how your body (and mind) will thank you.

. . . .

There is a direct connection
between self-nurturing
and self-respect.
—Julia Cameron

. . . .

Quick Tranquil Fixes

Taking time out of a hectic schedule to nurture your spirit may not be a possibility, especially when you're on deadline, running late to one of your many engagements or involved in a challenging conversation. Sometimes you just have a moment to turn chaos into calm:

Practice the three-part yogic breath. Practice at the office, while stuck in traffic, and during your luxurious evening home

Simply Be Meditation

Find a cozy, quiet place. Set an intention. Come to a comfortable cross-legged seated pose on a pillow, chair, yoga blanket, or meditation cushion. Close your eyes. Notice all the sensations around you—sounds, smells, breeze. Notice all the sensations inside you—tightness, heaviness, resistance. Observe your breath. Without judgment, practice being an observer of your mind. Allow yourself 3 to 5 minutes to settle in. Think of your thoughts like passing clouds. Don't hold on to them, and don't push them away. Just let them float across your mind's sky with recognition and detachment. Stay in tune with your breath throughout the journey. Feel the chest lifting and lowering with the breath. Incorporate a mantra such as "inner" on your inhale, and "peace" on your exhale to help you stay focused. Begin with 5 minutes and, with time, increase to 25-minute meditations. Release effort, release "the right way," and release expectations. Let this time be your chance to simply be.

alone reading. There is never a moment in the modern girl's life where this won't help. It's my personal lifesaving secret. Nothing helps you return to the present moment faster than breath awareness.

Open your shoulders. Driving, walking, shopping, cooking, writing, e-mailing—all these contribute to leaning forward and droopy shoulders. Counter this regularly to help prevent a closed and tight heart center. When you feel your heart sinking or your chest tightening, bring your arms behind your back, interlace your hands, and lift those arms up! Sway from side to side with the arms lifted, and feel the tension releasing. This tiny movement is sure to bring a skip back into your step and lighten your heavy load.

Tranquil Tip: Take shoulder opening a step deeper by bending the elbows of clasped hands and taking the clasped hands to the right hip as you squeeze the elbows in toward one another. Nope, they probably won't touch, but repeat on the other side and feel the shoulders come alive.

Spend $5 a Week on a "Luxury" Item
Reward yourself just for being you! A few of my favorite luxurious, yet not exorbitant, weekly treats are: • Lush bath bomb (www.lush.com) • hot-oil hair treatment from a local drugstore • a spiral-bound notebook to capture thoughts • a glossy magazine • candied almonds • bubble gum lip gloss • a fresh-baked cookie • fancy soap • bamboo starter stalk • a box of pomegranate green tea • a mango smoothie • a gardenia-scented votive candle • a pen with colored ink • a flakey croissant • an iced soy chai latte

Giving to yourself in this simple manner can help provide positive reinforcement for all the baby steps you're taking each week in the direction of your dreams.

Roll out your yoga mat. Even a five-minute block of open space can provide just enough tranquility to help you get your day back on track. Sometimes simply sitting or lying down on your mat with your eyes closed can do wonders to recharge you. If none of these are appealing to you at the moment, choose your favorite pose—pigeon, down dog, standing forward fold—and just breathe there for a few minutes. Taking the time to move out of your head and into your body is a sure quick fix.

Personalizing Your Self-Care

Build a solid relationship with yourself by practicing kindness and giving respect to all that you do. Get back in touch with the unadulterated delights you crave. Are you a die-hard movie lover? Go alone to a matinee and you won't have to share your Red Vines. Do you regret not spending enough time in your garden? Make it a priority and get your hands dirty. Make small changes in your routine that guarantee you space to savor the abundant simple pleasures that surround you. Life is full of hidden treasures. Let this be your first step toward carving out a life grounded in self-nurturing that serves you and others beyond what you thought possible. Go ahead girls, you're worth it!

. . . .

Caring for myself is not self-indulgence, it is self-preservation.
—Audre Lorde

. . . .

Omwork

Review your wheel of life and note areas where you want to raise a low score. List 5 steps you can take over the next week or month to increase your satisfaction in this area. How can you begin to convert your current life into your ideal life with a focus on your vision?

Resolve to indulge in at least one small self-nurturing act each week. That's 52 a year at minimum. Begin right now. No excuses.

Pull out your journal. How can you incorporate this sacred tool into your daily routine? Use it as an idea book. Carry a small spiral-bound notebook in your purse to pull out when the muse hits. Write as soon as you open your eyes in the morning and watch what pours out of your sleepy head. Find ways to incorporate this therapeutic tool into your regular self-care regime.

Savvy Sources

Read

Simple Abundance: A Daybook of Comfort and Joy, by Sarah Ban Breathnach

Gift from the Sea, by Anne Morrow Lindbergh

The Woman's Comfort Book: A Self-Nurturing Guide for Restoring Balance in Your Life, by Jennifer Louden

The Woman's Retreat Book: A Guide to Restoring, Rediscovering, and Reawakening Your True Self—in a Moment, an Hour, or a Weekend, by Jennifer Louden

A Voice of Her Own: Women and the Journal-Writing Journey, by Marlene Schiwy

Imagine a Woman in Love with Herself: Embracing Your Wisdom and Wholeness, by Patricia Lynn Reilly

Meditation Secrets for Women: Discovering Your Passion, Pleasure, and Inner Peace, by Camille Maurine and Lorin Roche

Girls' Night In: Spa Treatments at Home, by Jennifer Worick

Yin Yoga: Outline of a Quiet Practice, by Paul Grilley

Visit

www.comfortqueen.com

www.simpleabundance.com

www.what-fun.com

www.lush.com

Listen

Afterglow, by Sarah McLachlan

Tales of a Librarian: A Tori Amos Collection, by Tori Amos

Both Sides Now, by Joni Mitchell

Come Away with Me, by Norah Jones

Songbird, by Eva Cassidy

In between Dreams, by Jack Johnson

Baroque at Bathtime: A Relaxing Serenade to Wash Your Cares Away, by J. S. Bach et al.

Chapter 6

Creative Connection

nourish your inner artist

. . . .

I am my own experiment.

I am my own work of art.

—MADONNA

A hip tranquil chick's mantra is "Imagine, inspire, and innovate." Without imagination it is hard to allow yourself to dream. Without inspiration each day can seem devoid of meaning. Without innovation it is easy to stagnate. Take Madonna, for example: her ability to innovate has kept her in the spotlight for more than two decades with personas that run from controversial sex goddess to English mum writing children's books. The ability to imagine bigger things, a willingness to repot yourself to allow room to grow, and the courage to step outside the box are traits that help you stand out in a crowd and keep you excited about life.

When you find yourself complaining about a stagnant situation, entrust your journal, alone time, and yoga mat to bring clarity to your next steps. By working to bring growth into your daily life through reading something out of the ordinary, trying a new scent, or exploring a variation on a favorite pose, you'll be able to coddle your artistic nature and continue your creative streak. If you're doing your inner work, what appears to be stagnation is simply a seed germinating below the surface. A beautiful flower will bloom after the proper amount of nurturing and preparation. Let your imagination, inspiration, and innovation flourish.

. . . .

There are no days in life so memorable as those which vibrated to some stroke of the imagination.

—RALPH WALDO EMERSON

. . . .

Imagine This

Although you may have been discouraged from daydreaming as a child, this simple act can be life changing. If a girl can't imagine or dream, how can she possibly create? A big thinker would never get stuck on small visions. The world needs dreamers to perceive the impossible. Let's explore ways to begin imagining your life beyond its current walls.

Defining Life as Art

Each and every day we are given a new beginning. Don't just rely on Yom Kippur or New Year's to begin anew—you're given 365 fresh days each year, not just one! If you begin to think of your life as a work of art, each brushstroke, each decision, each player, each piece, has significant value. Every aspect makes you a unique work of art that can never be replicated.

Envisioning your life as the start of a masterpiece, let your canvas unfold into an image that makes you proud. If you don't like what you see, change the thick brushstrokes in your work to make them lighter. For example, if work is taking up too much of your life, explore ways to regain more balance. Or make the light brushstrokes for relationships bolder to give them a higher priority. Notice the areas where you'd like to see changes and use your artistic flair to make them happen. If you see a family in your future, visualize it on the canvas. If you see yourself sailing around the world with a significant other, paint it in

. . . .

We need to remember that
we are all created creative.
—Maya Angelou

. . . .

Play with Possibilities

Take a moment to let go of inhibitions and bring your inner child out to play.

1. If you could lead various lives during your lifetime, what would you choose? Astronaut, circus contortionist, actress, romance writer, cabaret singer, flight attendant, stylist, painter, sculptor, mother, cowgirl, nun, snowboard instructor, museum curator, school teacher, go-go dancer, pop star?
2. Why did you choose those lives?

Excitement, change, location, environment?

3. What appealed to you most? Fame, performance, creativity, solitude?
4. Ponder ways to bring aspects of these eccentric personalities into your current lifestyle. Start with a writing, art, dance, or acting class. Explore a move to a part of the country where that life is possible, or an informational interview of someone in the field.

vibrant hues. If you see yourself building an Oprah-esque empire, make sure it is prominently displayed. You control your artistic touches. You are given a fresh canvas every day to repaint with a renewed outlook. Enjoy the evolution of this masterpiece and cultivate creativity in all you do.

Backyard Inspiration

The opportunities for inspiration are sprinkled throughout your everyday activities. It is all a matter of perspective. Instead of viewing your barren patio as an eyesore, see it as an opportunity to connect with nature and create an outdoor retreat filled with thriving plants. Instead of viewing your boss's request to draft a memo to the founder of your company as a fear-inducing activity, view it as welcome challenge and a chance to get yourself in front of the company's visionary. Open yourself to inspiration through tapping into what is inside you and what might be waiting just outside your doorstep.

> The power of imagination
> makes us infinite.
> —John Muir

Revamp the Routine

To keep your inner artist inspired, give yourself space to listen to your inner voice and time to play. Both of these can be hard to fit into an already jam-packed schedule. However, without creating this space, life will become a series of blah to-dos. When you're feeling more like Debbie Downer than Holly Golightly, give yourself some time to renew

your spirit. When you're feeling stagnant and in need of a frivolously fun change of pace, take time to indulge in one of the suggested creative excursions. By adding spice to routine, and engaging in something new, you will jump-start a creative mindset that makes life interesting each and every day.

> Life is either a daring
> adventure or nothing at all.
> —Helen Keller

Creative Detours

Create a collage. This activity is sure to inspire you for months, or even years, to come. Make this a seasonal activity when you can carve out a few free hours. Have a refreshing spritzer nearby, good tunes playing, and enough room to get messy. Peruse your magazines and tear out images, quotes, or words that appeal to you. Take all the time you need and don't question why a bowl of vibrant green apples is enticing. Just rip it out. Once you've gone through all your magazines, look over your choices and notice what theme(s) emerge. During one retreat I led, a woman noticed that all her images had something to do with travel, and she realized that it was time for her to take a much-needed vacation.

 Tranquil Tip: A collage can be a powerful tool to bring what is unconscious to the forefront. Think of your collage as a visual map of your ideal, what you need, or what you're drawn to at this time. Reflect on ways you can bring more of what you created visually into your current reality. For example, if you chose lots of fashion images, ponder how you can bring

Take notice when your plants have outgrown their pots and need repotting. Keeping a plant in a pot past its prime can have devastating consequences. Similarly, when you've outgrown a job, relationship, or situation, it may be best to move on so you can continue to flourish.

Create a new yoga sequence. Rather than pulling out the same DVD or CD you always use or moving through sequences such as Surya Namaskar A or B that are old hat for you, make up your own sequence. Play with starting in relaxation or in bridge pose. Take it to pigeon and keep playing. The beauty of vinyasa is that it embodies a truly creative spirit. Let your body dance in and out of poses. Write down what worked or didn't work. Voilà—you've now created your very own sequence!

more style into your life. Or if you chose images of peaceful surroundings, or an organized environment, reflect on how you can begin creating an oasis for yourself.

Plant (or repot) something. Taking the time to get my hands dirty by digging in soil can be so grounding. A favorite time of the year for me is when impatiens arrive on the market in April. This beautifully blooming plant requires little care beyond water and gives me bursts of color until the first frost. Another option is buying seeds, small terra cotta pots (which can be painted in vibrant colors), and soil. As the little seedling pushes through the soil, you are reminded of nurturing your own growth process. The struggle from idea (seed) to blossom (dream realized) is a trés delicate journey that needs constant attention. Even if you don't have outdoor space beyond a windowsill, planting something will not only add life to your surroundings, but also reconnect you to a sense of growth.

Stepping Out

Inspiration can be found in your city's skyline, the blooming bush you pass on your way to work, the twinkling lights and sounds during the holidays, or the art in your company's lobby. To help you revamp your routine to dive into these sources of inspiration, below are a few of my stepping out secrets.

Indulge in armchair adventures. Maybe you don't have the finances to backpack through Europe or the time to devote to trekking through America's national parks.

. . . .

We must become alert enough to consciously replenish our creative resources as we draw on them.
—Julia Cameron

. . . .

The great news is that you can begin traveling by reading about someone else's adventures in the comfort of your own cozy chair. Sure you'll miss the full effect (along with the expenses, culture shock, and dirty laundry), but you can still gain insights from the escapade. Play exotic tunes associated with the region you're reading about. Eat food popular in your travel destination. For example, if you're "exploring" the Amalfi coast of Italy, listen to a Puccini opera, cook your favorite pasta dish, and dive into the adventures of a fellow femme.

 Tranquil Tip: For more inspiration, read the essays in *More Women Travel* (edited by Natania Jansz and Miranda Davies), *The Road Within* (edited by Sean O'Reilly et al.), *A Woman's Path* (edited by Lucy McCauley), and *A Woman's World* (edited by Marybeth Bond).

Connect to nature. The shedding of leaves in fall is a beautiful reminder to let go of things that are no longer working for us. The dead of winter serves as encouragement to hibernate, slow down, and go within. The blooming of spring is a gentle reminder to coax forth what was lying dormant during our winter hibernation. The vibrancy of summer offers us the opportunity to shine brightly and explore new territories. The seasons encourage us to remember that life is cyclical. Let nature inspire you to let go, rest, bloom, and glisten.

Heart art. Have you ever walked through a museum or attended a concert and felt so stirred that you pulled out a sketchpad or signed up for singing lessons? Exposure to other people's art on a regular basis is sure to stimulate you. Stroll through the botanical gardens. Admire a local art exhibit. Visit a coffeehouse concert. Attend a book signing to chat with the author. Read about the artistic process. When you surround yourself with other creative people, you will find that the inspiration rubs off.

 Tranquil Tip: Make it a point to support friends or colleagues who are living their creative dreams by attending their functions: a play, an opening, or a reading. It takes courage to put yourself out there, and your presence is sure to be appreciated. Plus it will get your creativity flowing!

Innovation

An invention or a new way of doing things sums up the art of innovation. Without innovation life becomes stale, stagnant, drab, and dull. Who wants that? Explore experiences

> Innovation is the creation of the new or the re-arranging of the old in a new way.
> —Michael Vance

out of your comfort zone to shake things up. If you have been working in the same field for years and feel unfulfilled, why not consider going back to school or if you have the skills, start applying to that dream job? When the city no longer excites you and you fantasize about living on an acre of land with a lake, take steps to make that a reality. Are you typically a closeted journal writer? Start a blog and share your thoughts with the world. Infuse some mystery and spontaneity into that groove and watch those creative juices bubble up inside!

Being prepared for creative action at all times is part of the hip tranquil chick path.

Carry your journal to record random musings. • Always have your yoga mat handy. • Create a craft basket filled with glue sticks, watercolors, stickers, construction paper, paintbrushes, ribbons, remnant fabric, and scented markers. • Stock up with party supplies such as toile napkins, frozen hors d'oeuvres, chocolate truffles, wine, and great tunes so you can throw together a small soirée in no time. • Build up a basket filled with candles, picture frames, bath products, and girly must-haves for on-the-fly gift giving. • Collect chic stationery, celebratory note cards, and a stash of stamps so the "thinking of you" letter is at your fingertips.

Risk Equals Reward

Risk taking encompasses pushing your boundaries and saying yes when no feels more comfortable. When I had just finished my first yoga teacher training, I got a call from a teacher asking if I would sub her class. My initial reaction was to scream "No way!" and hang up, but instead I said, "Of course," and anxiously awaited the challenge. My teaching career launched thanks to that one tiny courageous choice. Taking risks that push you outside your safe and comfortable zone helps you grow in a powerful way.

. . . .

We will only understand the
miracle of life fully when we allow
the unexpected to happen.
—PAULO COELHO

. . . .

Risks	=	Reward
Submit an application to a summer program abroad.	=	Explore another country.
Take three months off in between jobs.	=	Travel and get to know yourself.
Try a handstand at the wall.	=	Get closer to finding your balance.
Raise your hand to give input on a project.	=	Get known as a go-getter.
Volunteer to head the annual gala.	=	Gain experience in event planning and rub elbows with those in charge.
Submit a proposal to a book agent.	=	Receive feedback on your work and possibly gain a cheerleader.
Launch an online business.	=	Become your own boss.

Do It Differently

Rather than simply trying something new, do something you always do, but do it differently. Instead of sipping chamomile tea, go crazy with jasmine. Instead of respond-

. . . .

The world needs dreamers and the
world needs doers. But above all,
the world needs dreamers who do.
—Sarah Ban Breathnach

. . . .

ing to e-mails as soon as they come in, check a few times a day and respond in chunks. Instead of sending a fruit basket to your grandmother for the holidays, send a live wreath wrapped with a bow in her favorite color. Instead of taking power yoga, indulge in yin yoga. Instead of reading chick lit, read a classic that you flubbed through in school. Instead of ordering cucumber maki rolls, order cucumber mixed with avocado rolls.

By making small changes to what is already part of your routine, you can take a creative detour with minimal effort and interruption to your casually chic lifestyle.

Cultivate Creativity

Creativity surrounds you. Through the way you talk and the way you listen and the everyday choices you make in your work, dress, home, friends, and food, you are able to connect with creativity. Make conscious choices that allow you to sparkle, grow, and change in a way that radi-

ates your most fabulous self. Breathing life into the mundane offers the opportunity to reinvigorate yourself each and every day. Be mindful of the sounds of the ocean, birds in flight, the color of the yoga mat you use, and the beauty of the shoe section of Saks. Infuse your life with creative awareness and watch your own artistic canvas continue to grow into a priceless masterpiece.

. . . .

Creativity is inventing,
experimenting, growing, taking
risks, breaking rules, making
mistakes, and having fun.
—Mary Lou Cook

. . . .

Omwork

Make a list of 25 things you must do before you die. For example, jump out of a plane, snowboard, take a cruise, lead a workshop, direct a film, write a novel, green your office. Post this list in a prominent place, on note cards, or in a journal with associated illustrations.

Vow to express your creative and artistic self each day. Do this through your personal style and dress, what you read and listen to, how you talk and carry yourself. Mindfully make a point to do something that takes you past your edge daily.

Carve out at least four hours each month for creative expression. Try one of the suggested creative detours. Sign up for a drawing, painting, dance, photography, pottery, sculpting, decorating, sewing, knitting, music, or film class. Get a group of girlfriends together to transform your favorite tees into a halter, skirt, or leg warmer. Spend time planting and tending your garden, if only a single plant.

Savvy Sources

Read

The Artist's Way: A Spiritual Path to Higher Creativity, by Julia Cameron

12 Secrets of Highly Creative Women: A Portable Mentor, by Gail McMeekin

Living Out Loud: Activities to Fuel a Creative Life, by Keri Smith

Make Your Creative Dreams Real: A Plan for Procrastinators, Perfectionists, Busy People, and People Who Would Really Rather Sleep All Day, by SARK

The Woman's Book of Creativity, by C. Diane Ealy

Generation T: 108 Ways to Transform a T-shirt, by Megan Nicolay

Visit

www.planetsark.com
www.blogger.com
www.kerismith.com
www.paper-source.com
www.utrechtart.com
www.momastore.org

Listen

No Se Parece a Nada, by Albita

Confessions on a Dance Floor, by Madonna

A Mozart Serenades Weekend, by Wolfgang Amadeus Mozart

Tchaikovsky at Tea Time: A Refreshing Blend for Body and Spirit, by Tchaikosvky

La Llorona, by Lhasa De Sela

Musicology, by Prince

Lounging at the Nick at Niteclub, by various artists

The outer conditions of a
person's life will always be found
to reflect their inner beliefs.

—JAMES ALLEN

Outer Chic

Once you connect to your inner
chic, your outer world will also
become "chic-ified." By taking your
practice beyond the poses and
delving into your internal processes,
your outer world will glow through
conscious relationships, a prosperous
profession, and financial finesse.

Chapter 7

Refined Relations

sexy socializing and community culture

Keep away from people who

try to belittle your ambitions.

—MARK TWAIN

Surrounding yourself with supportive connections is a must for the hip tranquil chick. You may be new to a city or a job, newly single, or simply looking to expand your circle. Either way, locate symbiotic souls by putting yourself out there. Get clear on what you want in a significant other, friends, and colleagues, and set out to find these people. As you take responsibility for creating your own reality, you'll find that relationships are no exception. By connecting with others who share your passions, a hip tranquil chick can do great things and throw some fabulous fêtes along the way.

No one can make you feel
inferior without your consent.
—ELEANOR ROOSEVELT

Chic and Conscious Connections

Birds of a feather do truly flock together. Surround yourself with people who inspire you. Some people leave you feeling energized and filled with possibility after a quick tea date. Yet others can leave you feeling defeated and exhausted after a five-minute phone call. Our time and energy are sacred, so honor that by building the kinds of relationships that bring out the best in you and others. By defining who you want in your life, developing your communication style, and adding special touches to your interactions, you'll notice that strong and supportive connections will lift you up and help you shine.

Locate Like-Minded Pals

The search for similarly minded folks can be tricky once you leave school and venture out on your own. When I first moved to Washington, D.C., I wondered how I'd meet people beyond my beau-of-the-moment. I found a local sorority alumnae group, joined the regional paralegal association, attended various conferences, visited the surround- ing yoga studios, and tried out a meditation class. I met a few people at these events, but I still longed for more of a community. You know, that special feeling of belonging to a group. How to find this in a big ol' city?

· · · · · · · · · · · · · · · · · · · ·

Nobody sees a flower really; it is so small. We haven't time, and to see takes time—like to have a friend takes time.
—Georgia O'Keefe

· · · · · · · · · · · · · · · · · · · ·

It may feel daunting at times, but the point is to keep putting yourself out there, meet friends of friends, and explore the social opportunities that your community offers.

 Tranquil Tip: When building your community, never say no to an invite and make up your mind to have a great time, even at your new pal's birthday bash for her Bichon. Remember, community is all about building connections, supporting others, and making selective choices when it flourishes.

Creating Community

Don't wait for things to come to you. You're a busy girl! Go out and make things happen. The options are endless, but it is crucial that you step outside your comfort zone in order to connect with the many rewards that await you.

The artist: Sign up for a drawing class and make a date to practice between classes with the girl sitting next to you. Attend a gallery opening and strike up a conversation with a person admiring your favorite piece.

The activist: Nothing fixes loneliness quite like doing something for others. Volunteer to support a cause that's meaningful to you—a youth program, a homeless shelter, an assisted living center, or the humane society.

The entrepreneur: Start a business that will attract the community you are seeking. Seek out mentors and assist mentees. Join business groups, Toastmasters, and networking groups to help grow your inner circle.

The seeker: Ask your new friends to introduce you to their pals. Join a yoga, meditation, synagogue, or church community to meet other spiritually minded people. Sign up for a personal growth retreat.

The fitness fanatic: Join your local climbing gym and begin trekking out into the great outdoors with your newfound friends. Sign up for a 10K run or a marathon and ask for a training buddy. Venture onto the bike path and be friendly to fellow cyclists—ask about gatherings or clubs.

The techie: Connect with people who have similar interests online through Friendster, MySpace, or one of the many other online communities. Start a blog or podcast and watch your connections grow globally.

The literary: Put up a flier at the local library or artsy bookstore to start a book club. Show up at poetry readings and book signings. Get to know your independent bookstore staff.

Throw a Swanky Soirée

The hip tranquil chick is the queen of soirée throwing on a budget, on a moment's notice, and even in her tiny one-bedroom apartment. What better way to create refined relations

and cultivate conscious connections than through hosting a party? It's a great way to bring a few friends together, to reciprocate their hospitality, and—if they bring their own friends—to grow your community in one fell swoop.

 Tranquil Tip: When inviting pals to an intimate affair, avoid mingling your beau's rugby team with your Ayn Rand book club group and dog-park friends. Make sure the group is compatible or this faux pas may make for a very long and uncomfortable dinner.

Festive Fête Ideas

Being a hip hostess with the mostess lies in weaving a creative theme with tranquil touches. Here are a few of my quintessential celebrations:

Karma party. Ask everyone to bring a specific suggested donation for a featured charity. Have a speaker from the charity or special cause give a spiel about the organization and mingle with the partygoers. Display paraphernalia from the charity for pals to pick up, or fanned out in creative place holders or frames. For example, when I collaborate with the humane society, they bring handouts on their mission and stickers for pet owners to put on their doors or windows to alert others of the animal's presence in case of an emergency. Combine this awareness-raising event with a celebration such as a fashion show, black-tie gala with dogs, or book launch at a posh lounge to pull it all together in an uplifting, supportive fashion. Be creative and watch your karma points soar.

Tranquil Tip: Karma parties can be done on a very small budget by getting local food and beverage organizations to contribute to the cause as sponsors, or by buying in bulk and offering simple savories and non-alcoholic bubblies, and the price of admission can be a can of food to donate to a local shelter.

Celebratory party. Birthdays and baby showers are so traditional. Celebrate unique milestones such as bon voyages, promotions, reunions, open houses, changing seasons, a new pair of Manolos—anything you deem celebration worthy. Throw yourself a shower when you buy your first home or get that fabulous new gig.

Tranquil Tip: Each hip tranquil chick has an annual affair everyone looks forward to. Whether it's a Black and White gala on New Year's, Halloween extravaganza, or an annual springtime picnic in the park, develop a signature event that will keep people buzzing.

Chick clique. Let your inner child play by inviting your closest gal pals over for chick-flick watching (*When Harry Met Sally*, *Sleepless in Seattle*), a clothing swap, journal writing, a yoga session, going over the latest *Real Simple* or fall edition of *Vogue*, or a pamper party using home-based facial recipes. For special gatherings, kick it up a notch and bring in a professional: a psychic to do readings, a salsa instructor, or a makeup artist for a group lesson.

Meet and greet. Host a local author, politician, or community leader to help build awareness and community. Establish your-self as a girl with a finger on the pulse. It also builds goodwill and allows you to be a catalyst for connections within your community.

Trunk shows. Host your fave local designer and invite your girlfriends over for a sneak peek at her fabulous wares. Or host numerous designers, have postcards made to distribute around town, invite the press, and set up a seasonal shoppe at your home where local designers can showcase their creativity, guests can nibble on crudités, and you can relish in creating a community that supports other women's art.

Costume party. Be creative: invite guests to come as their favorite writer, most inspiring performer, or their future self. This allows guests to enjoy the playfulness of dress-up in a more sophisticated setting. I once dressed up as Anaïs Nin for a costume party, and this stimulated fascinating conversations with the literary lovers in the crowd.

Drop the Entertaining Drama

When teaching yoga, I think of it as theater—sound, smell, touch, and sight create powerful experiences. Think "theater" when inviting your special ones into your home. The ability to host an intimately savvy soirée is a skill worth pulling off well, and no reason is needed other than the desire to connect. What hip tranquil chick doesn't want that? The key is to host these events with grace and to enjoy your time with the guests. Preparing a timeline and a complete shopping list, enlisting help, and having a cavalier attitude can help avoid drama. Keep the mood light, the drinks flowing, the guests chatting, and the music playing. Relish in what you create by putting together a very simple, cheap chic, and elegant extravaganza.

Tranquil Tip: Don't forget why you're hosting the soirée. Greet and say farewell to each guest, introduce them to one another, and work the room to make those conscious connections you're seeking. Guests will remember these exchanges more than if the ice bucket stayed full.

Adorable Add-ons

Put your stylish signature on everything you touch, and make others feel special through your creative connection to the art of detail. Here are my signature touches for making an event sparkle.

Gifts: Toss festive confetti into invitations or welcome cards containing a handwritten note. Give colorful gift bags filled with treats that nurture their senses, such as scented candles, or that encourage self-care, such as bath salts. Even a thoughtfully wrapped piece of quality chocolate or personalized cookie will feel like a luxurious treat.

Décor: Wrap vibrant ribbons around stemware. Don't forget the bathroom—little bud vases with gerber daisies are a sweet touch. Sprinkle rose petals around the focus table. Ensure an abundance of sassy cocktail napkins (leopard print are my fave). Incorporate a theme: for example, have a focus table with framed postcard images and travel books if it is a bon voyage party.

Mood: Play festive music to help set the stage. World beat, lounge, and salsa tunes get your guests moving. Be sure to amp it up to maintain the mood as the night goes on. Low lighting helps hide the lack of time you had to clean and creates a chill vibe. Strategically placed white candles are sure to set the mood.

Savories: If you stick with finger foods, you don't have to wash dishes. Comforting snack foods such hummus and baked pita bread, kalamata olives, fresh berries, and mini-cupcakes make your guests feel at home. *Bon appétit!* Special-order fortune cookies with your favorite inspirational quotes inside. Think simple, savory, and seasonal. For example, simmering apple cider on your stovetop is a great mood setter for the holidays. Sparkling water with floating raspberries and small cubes of watermelon is a refresher for the warmer months. And don't forget a beautiful presentation. Simple savories appear more spectacular when offered in a gorgeous china bowl or fancy tray with doilies and garnishes such as rosemary sprigs, a peeled lemon skin, or sliced strawberry.

Maintaining and Nurturing Affairs

The hip tranquil chick is that girl who men and women alike want to befriend, who lights up a room when she walks in, and who is never too busy for thoughtful gestures. It takes one skill set to attract and begin a relationship, yet it requires a whole other skill set to maintain and nurture relationships in a healthy way.

For the busy girl-on-the-go, it can become another to-do to call a girlfriend, check in with Mom, make out with your beau, and

> Love is the only satisfactory answer to the problem of human existence.
> —ERICH FROMM

walk the dog. However, these connections with other people in your life will help keep you sane. Some of my girlfriends and I will schedule months ahead just to grab dinner or meet for tea, but we're sure to make it a priority, or otherwise everyday minutiae will fill the empty spaces. Become proactive about sustaining healthy relationships through thoughtful "I'm thinking of you" gestures and scheduled quality time. Taking a relationship for granted is sure to cause a breakdown along the way.

Sacred and Sexy Socializing

Take the time to do small, considerate gestures. This allows for a continual connection even when you're not together physically and touches others in a sacred way.

Girlfriends: Cut out an article that you know she would enjoy reading. • For a friend who just had a baby, drop off ready-made meals like homemade soup or a pasta salad that she can store in the fridge. • Instead of a hat-and-glove set for the holidays, give the gift of two registrations for a knitting workshop, or a meditation series. That way you can spend time together connecting through the experience. • Get two tickets to an exhibit your friend has been dying to see. • Ask if she needs anything when she's under the weather. Or better yet, drop by with a box of tea, flowers, orange juice, and fresh fruit. • Arrange for child care for a girlfriend in need of some serious retail therapy or yoga practice, and whisk her away for some self-care/girl time.

Loved ones: Call your grandma just to say hello. • Remember birthdays. • Send an electronic "thinking of you" card. • Send candy and a thoughtful note via snail mail. Sending anything via snail mail these days is sure to be appreciated. • Leave a sweet Post-It note on a loved one's computer, bathroom door, or suitcase prior to traveling. • When your family calls, be present and listen.

Colleagues: Leave seasonal chocolates or candles in the employee lounge as a constant thank you for their efforts. • Create a team basket for your staff filled with pick-me-ups to help keep their energy strong—pretzels, raisins, trail mix, and peanut butter crackers. • Tuck a sweet "thank you for being you" card on your colleague's keyboard. • Bring back gifts for your team from your travels.

Communication

We all know this, but it can't be emphasized enough: communication is key to any relationship. Almost every time I pass people chatting on their cell phones, it seems as if they're complaining about somebody. I wonder what would happen if they shared their frustration with the person that they were upset with, rather than a third party. How much quicker and easier would we be able to resolve conflict, misunderstandings, or false assumptions? Yet sometimes we simply need to process a situation or feeling before confronting it in the heat of the moment. Thank goodness for reflection time and learning to pick your battles!

 Tranquil Tip: Reaching out to a long-lost BFF can do wonders to revitalize your sense of connection to a larger community. It is so joyful to have giggles with someone who knew you so well way back when, especially if you've recently relocated. Reconnect to someone today that you miss!

> To effectively communicate, we must realize that we are all different in the way we perceive the world.
> —ANTHONY ROBBINS

Compromise

All relationships must contain an element of compromise. They are a blend of give and take. What may seem like petty differences of opinion at the beginning of a relationship are sure to lead to bigger concerns when they involve children or decisions about where to live, how to manage a business, or how

> It is well to give when asked, but it is better to give unasked through understanding.
> —KAHLIL GIBRAN

to incorporate religion into your lives. How you handle compromise will help shape the future of your relationships. Make sure that you recognize when you're taking advantage

Observe Your Communication Style
Are you a pouter, worst-case-scenario assumer, confronter, or avoider? By identifying your communication style, you're sure to find improvement on numerous levels. For example, I have always been a pouter. When hurt, I would stew about it for hours and when asked, "What's wrong?" replied with "Nothing." Finally my karma came back to bite me when I dated a pouter. Needless to say, we never got anywhere. I've since learned to assess a situation, process my feelings, and discuss them with my friend, partner, or colleague immediately. This helps to short-circuit the "Nothing" response complete with an extended lower lip.

of friends or when you're being taken advantage of ("Sure, I'll work my tenth weekend in a row"). Set boundaries and compromise when necessary. One of my favorite mantras is "Edges pushed, boundaries held." Explore outside your comfort zone so that you continue growing, but be sure to maintain your boundaries in all relationships.

 **Tranquil Tip:** Do you always find yourself meeting your beau on his side of town rather than your stomping ground? Do you find yourself meeting friends for Thai when you prefer Mexican? Do you join your girlfriend for Ashtanga when you prefer Anusara? Meditate on the ways you compromise and explore where you can make a change.

. . . .

The river that flows in you
also flows in me.
—KABIR

. . . .

Commitment

Sometimes a relationship is fleeting and a part of your life for a short time. Another is worth holding on to and feeds your soul for years to come. When you find such a relationship, be sure to do what is necessary to keep it going even if you live in different parts of the country. Having a longtime history with a trusted gal pal can be comforting when you're battling an issue you've been discussing with her since junior high.

I've seen many friends fall off the radar after giving birth, getting married, moving, or starting a business. Friends often understand, especially if you ask for their patience and articulate you're in the throes of a big change but will be back in touch soon. Remember that relationships are a two-way street, and complaining that so-and-so never calls is not fair if you, too, are not reaching out.

Commitment Etiquette
Honor the implied commitment you have to those close to you by valuing their time and their contributions to who you have become. • Make it a priority to remember birthdays and other dates close to your loved one's hearts. (Sign up for free reminders at birthdayalarm.com.) • Pick up a goodie bag filled with an organic onsie, parenting books, and bath salts for your girlfriend who is a new mother and snail-mail it to her. • When you make a date with a friend, keep it. • Know when to let a relationship go, and do so with grace.

Consciousness

Bringing mindfulness into a relationship helps you consciously create the relationship you're seeking while also staying in tune with your needs and desires. Regular reflection on your relationships will ensure that you're being true to who you are and that you're able to nurture the relationships you choose to be in. By embracing consciousness with a partner, family member, or neighbor, you are committing to a deeper relationship. For example, I recently saw a business acquaintance featured in an online magazine story. I sent her a congratulatory e-mail and we decided to meet for lunch. During our lunch we explored the numerous challenges of running a business, exchanged advice, and shared ideas. We were able to move beyond simple niceties and create a conscious connection based on mutual experiences.

 Tranquil Tip: Take your relationships beyond "Hi, how are you?" and into a deeper level of expression. • Offer words of wisdom to a struggling apprentice. • Ask your employer how she is doing and really listen. • Let a friend know the artistic potential you see in her work. • Thank your beau for loving you, idiosyncrasies and all.

We are not here to fix, change or belittle another person. We are here to support, forgive and heal one another.
—MARIANNE WILLIAMSON

Refined Relations

Nothing stretches us quite like our interactions with others. Surround yourself with people who embody your values as well as those who encourage you to think bigger. Enjoy the exchange of energy that happens when you become part of a community larger than yourself. Refined relations encompass integrity, compassion, and fun. Be sure you're enjoying yourself on this wild ride.

Even after all this time the sun never says to the earth "You owe me." Look what happens with a love like that—it lights the whole world.
—HAFIZ

Omwork

Reflect on your top 10 relationships. Are you happy in them? What is lacking or what would help them grow? Can you carve out more space for these relationships, or are they taking up too much space? Do you find yourself drained, or excited and energized, when around them?

Explore ways to make real connections with others. Find local organizations that are aligned with your values and interests. Seek out others on a similar path. Sign up for various listservs, read local magazines, and newspapers. If your unique interest doesn't have an organized community, create it or join a similarly minded group virtually!

Make necessary changes to stop negative patterns. Do you overwork so that you're never able to attend social events? Do you resist invitations out of fear? Do you constantly rebound from romantic relationships to avoid being alone? Observe your patterns and begin making changes to your relationships to support ample amounts of sexy socializing and the building of a solid community culture.

Savvy Sources

Read

A Woman's Worth, by Marianne Williamson

Grow, the Modern Woman's Handbook: How to Connect with Self, Lovers, and Others, by Lynne Franks

For Goddess' Sake: Get the Girls Together and Have Some Fun, by Hailey D. D. Klein

The Last-Minute Party Girl: Fashionable, Fearless, and Foolishly Simple Entertaining, by Erika Lenkert

A Home for the Heart: Creating Intimacy and Community in Our Everyday Lives, by Charlotte Sophia Kasl

If the Buddha Dated: A Handbook for Finding Love on a Spiritual Path, by Charlotte Sophia Kasl

Girl Group Confidential: The Ultimate Guide to Starting, Running and Enjoying Your Own Women's Group, by Jennifer Worick

Visit

www.evite.com   www.myspace.com
www.classmates.com   www.friendster.com

Listen

Music to Make Love to Your Old Lady By, by Loveage

The Mirror Conspiracy, by Thievery Corporation

Solarium Delirium, by Cirque du Soleil

Tanto Tempo Remixes, by Bebel Gilberto

Asfalto: Street Tango, by Pablo Ziegler

Todos los Romances, by Luis Miguel

Greatest Hits, by Air Supply

Moon Safari, by AIR

Chapter 8

Professional Prosperity

consciously carve your career path

· ·

Everyone has been made for some particular work,

and the desire for that work has been put in our hearts.

—RUMI

Making a living and spending a significant portion of your life in a profession means that finding a field you're passionate about is a must. A hip tranquil chick thrives on sharing her creative spirit through work and seeks career choices that allow this process to unfold naturally.

A continual evaluation of your skills, strengths, and weaknesses, and the areas in which you thrive, is important in order for you to stay in tune with your limitless possibilities. The exploration of your métier will enable you to unearth endless opportunities. A hip tranquil chick may design handbags for a few years, head to Guatemala to help build schools for a few months, and return home to become a freelance travel writer. The paths are many. Set your sails. Let's go!

Trademark Paralegal to Tranquility Maven

When I realized that I was looking forward to retirement only one year after graduating from college, I knew I needed to take matters into my own hands. Having read every self-discovery, journal writing, and yoga book I could get my hands on, I signed up for yoga teacher training, and turned my fourth-floor-walk-up living room into a yoga studio.

Okay, I confess I've had a couple of dreams over the past seven years of returning to a secure law firm job in which I work from 9 to 5, have less fuss, and maybe even enjoy a dose of free time, but I always wake up and am so grateful for what I have—drama and all. I want to inspire other women to grow, dream wildly, and make things happen. I want the studio to be a lifestyle oasis offering fabulous togs, spa treatments, and amazing yoga. In addition, I love growing the offerings to great lifestyle wear that's perfect for on the mat and on the town; blogging, podcasting, and writing this book to share ideas on being a hip, conscious, and tranquil modern girl; and exploring additional ways in which I can help spread tranquility through my non-profit The Tranquil Space Foundation. This is my passion and I feel blessed to have found it. What is yours?

. . . .
If you wish to achieve worthwhile things in your personal and career life, you must become a worthwhile person in your own self-development.

—BRIAN TRACY
. . . .

Savvy Skill Assessment

When exploring the ideal way to spend this huge portion of your life, you may visualize yourself on a beach with an umbrella drink as your ideal way to spend two-thirds of your waking life. However, reality, mortgage payments, and retirement planning make it important to dig deeper. Hopefully, finding a career that feeds your passion will be even more exciting than sitting on a white sand beach with your fave drink. OK, very close!

Consciously Carve the Perfect Profession

The perfect profession may feel as out of reach as a fairy tale, but I promise you that by using yoga to dive into your deepest desires, following the steps I give you, and allowing yourself the time to dream, you will be able to have a perfect position. It may even entail creating your own business!

Step 1: Network. In retail you always hear "location, location, location." For landing the perfect position, I think "network, network, network." I'm the first to admit that showing up at an event where I know no one and passing out my business card is not my thing. But I also know that there is great value in connecting with others and putting myself out there in a way that goes well beyond passing out a card.

. . . .
You know you are on the road to success if you would do your job and not be paid for it.

—OPRAH WINFREY
. . . .

Look for similar opportunities in your field of interest. Make it a point to arrive at these events with clear intentions, an open mind, and a jovial attitude. Look for someone that appears approachable. Introduce yourself, then ask for her story—what is her business, how long has she been a feng shui consultant, how does she find her clients? Letting other people talk about themselves (their

What Makes You Tick?

If "TGIF" is a weekly part of your vocabulary, explore the questions below to excavate how to wake up each day excited about your work.

1. **Review all your former jobs** from lemonade stand maven to Gap T-shirt folder to account executive. Note what you liked and didn't like about your varied positions. Create a "must have" and a "cannot bear" list for your ideal role.

2. Working from your two lists, **write out an ideal job description for your perfect role.** Be very clear, down to the benefits. Does it include a corner office, immersion in a creative environment, the ability to work from home, the chance to be outdoors, a matched 401(k), weekly brainstorming sessions with the CEO, or four weeks' paid vacation?

3. **What do you love to do in your free time?** Knitting, yoga, music, writing, decorating? Explore ways to incorporate your passions into a livelihood. If you love to knit, you might open a knitting store, offer knitting workshops in your home, import exotic yarn.

4. If you had an unlimited supply of money and didn't need to work, **what would you do with your time?** Explore ways to incorporate this activity into your livelihood.

5. **Ask your friends and family** what they see as your strengths and weaknesses. Sometimes those close to you will have valuable insights into who you are.

Once you've tallied up your answers, reflect on the skills associated with this ideal scenario. Do you need an MSW, a yoga teacher training, a crash course in design, an understanding of business operations? Begin researching programs, trainings, and internships. Gather all the details. Carefully weigh your options and determine your next steps.

favorite topic) can often help generate great ideas that translate into your profession. If you're hearing a speaker on a panel, make it a point to craft a question and approach her after her talk. You may meet a future business partner, a mentor, or a new fan. Join your local chamber of commerce, women's business center, women's social organization, and industry-related organization.

Tranquil Tip: Besides attending networking opportunities, why not try helping organize them? You can either launch your own event or volunteer your help for an existing one. This way you are guaranteed to rub elbows with key people like speakers and organizers.

Step 2: Go on Informational Interviews. Once you've met a few people through your networking, they are sure to know a friend of a friend that you could contact to set up an informational interview. These are usually short, sweet, one-hour interactions ideally over breakfast or lunch (your treat) where you can pick their brains on their industry, job, or company. Since most people need to break for a quick bite, asking to do it over a meal is a nice way to avoid cutting into their busy day and to offer them something in exchange.

If you aren't able to locate anyone but want to learn more about a particular company, call its human resources department to see if you can set up an informational interview. Be proactive and take your career to new heights with all sorts of inside scoop.

Step 3: Seek Out Internship Opportunities. Offering to work for free as an intern or at a low-level position is a guaranteed way to learn about a new industry and gain invaluable insights. Never feel as if you are above this often overlooked opportunity. Seeing the workings of an industry firsthand and working with big names in any capacity will jump-start your career, or at least help you determine if a particular business is for you. It also allows you to explore an industry without feeling beholden

if you decide it isn't for you. A girl who has an internship behind her looks like a real go-getter!

Step 4: Craft a Resourceful Résumé. Think of your résumé as a really good spa menu. You want the reader to know all the nitty-gritty in a clear and concise manner with verbiage that entices the potential employer to try you out. Sell yourself. Always have an up-to-date résumé on hand. Even if you love your current position, you never know when you'll be asked to share your stats. Create a new résumé for each job you're applying for to ensure that it is geared specifically to that role. Skip the objective at the top. We all know that you want "a rewarding and challenging position that utilizes your skills." Include interests only if it is a creative role you're applying for and they seem applicable. Be sure to list your USPs (unique selling points) throughout your descriptions of previous employment and education, and make sure they tie in with the company you're interested in.

Step 5: Be Creative in Your Cover Letter. Your cover letter should also evolve with each job for which you're applying. Employers love to see that you've done your homework. Mention how your values align with their mission, how the job description matches your skill set perfectly, and why you're seeking employment with their company. As an employer of numerous hip tranquil chicks, I'm always drawn to those cover letters that radiate attention to detail, creativity, thoughtfulness, and alignment with our message. Let this concise letter sell you to the company in an understated yet enticing manner.

Tranquil Tip: A hip tranquil chick sees beyond a typical cover letter and finds a way to showcase her talents. I know a graphic designer who was applying for a job in February, so she designed a special Valentine card that outlined the job description in a stylish heart with the headline "Be Mine." She then tucked her résumé inside the card. Yes, she got the gig!

Step 6: Entice the Interviewer. The interview is your chance to shine. You've pored over your pitch and hooked them with your résumé and cover letter. Now is your opportunity to show them your enthusiasm and your professionalism live and in person. Be sure to arrive prepared with questions, having perused their website and marketing materials as thoroughly as possible. Read the bios of those who are interviewing you, do a Google search on them, and ask them questions about something that caught your eye. This is your chance to show them why they should hire you, not your chance to waste their time bringing you up to speed on public information about the company.

During the interview, be sure to get clarity on the role for which you're applying. What is a typical day like? What are the company's goals and how does your role advance them? Will you have a mentor or trainer? What are the growth possibilities in the company? How can you help the company succeed?

Tranquil Tip: Dealing with the drama of an unfamiliar location or city parking can be very stressful, so allow yourself ample time to gather your thoughts at a nearby bookstore or café while sipping some herbal tea and reviewing your notes.

Step 7: Send a Thoughtful Thank You. This often-forgotten courtesy is a must-do in my book. It will set you apart, earn you good karma points, and is sure to leave a lasting impression with the interviewer. This is also your chance to have the last word. If you lack experience, emphasize your education and skill set. If you lack the education, emphasize your experience and skills that apply to the role. Send it on stationery that aligns with the company—bold and colorful for a creative job, conservative and traditional for a corporate job.

Strategic Steps to an "Overnight Success"

All righty, so we all know that overnight career success is not really possible. However, if you stack your cards right, you can become an heir to the professional princess throne.

Be a team player: Avoid office gossip. Participating in the drama is sure to quench your curiosity but tarnish your integrity. • Always consider the company's needs in addition to your own. Yes, staying late the fifth day in a row is upsetting because you keep missing your fave yoga time slot, but if your project has a deadline, being a team player with a good attitude is sure to get you noticed and rewarded. • Always attend company picnics and holiday parties and ensure that you're seen!

Be savvy: Practice smart e-mail etiquette. Inside jokes can be fun, but taking back a sent e-mail message is next to impossible. A good friend once told me never to write in an e-mail what I wouldn't want plastered on the front page of the *Washington Post*. • Seek additional training to help support your company's needs. • Ask to attend industry conferences and trade shows. Network within the industry. You never know where your next big lead will come from. • No longer passionate about your day job? Begin moonlighting and explore your entrepreneurial side.

Be bold: Never be shy about asking for additional compensation due to taking on increased responsibilities or winning a big client—know your value within the organization and let it be known. • Dress for the role that you want. You may be applying for the receptionist position so that you can learn more about the fashion industry, but dress as if you're applying for a senior-level position. Dress comfortably in a manner that aligns with the industry. Do your own research before your big day and stroll by the building during your lunch hour to see what people are wearing.

Be a leader: Show your leadership characteristics by speaking up at meetings, welcoming new hires, and mentoring an intern. • If you observe a co-worker complaining, jump in and brainstorm ways to remedy the situation. • When offered additional opportunities or projects, never let a chance pass you by. Challenging yourself and showing your ability to grow within your role is sure to leave a strong impression.

Mindful Moonlighting

When I took the leap into self-employment, I had been working full time and teaching yoga classes for almost a year before the double life became too much. Moonlighting is a perfect way to test the waters and ensure a new

venture is all you envision it to be. For example, if you long to start a dog-walking service but aren't ready to leave your day job, start after hours and on the weekend. See if you really love it and enjoy the administrative aspects that come along with keeping up with someone else's schedule, keys, and Fido's special needs. Maybe you dream of being behind the turntables at the biggest club in town. Spin tunes at your own party, and let your guests know that your services are available. You may begin to feel as if you're living a double life for a while, but this allows you the opportunity to strategically explore the plethora of options available to you.

On Your Own

Building a business is a lot like a yoga practice. Start by getting centered and grounded, slowly move into the flow, and ideally end with the ultimate yoga pose—relaxation. Here are tips on how you can create a business that corresponds with the flow of your favorite yoga practice. Remember to breathe!

Get centered: Here's where you begin to gather your resources. Do your market research, attend trainings, start moonlighting, create a business plan, make a list of the supplies you will need, conduct informational interviews, talk with others in the field.

Set an intention: Determine what you want and why you want it! Keep a focus on serving. Remember, all businesses are created to serve. Never lose sight of your intention. It will keep you going during long, long days.

Warm up: Get moving! Create a website, make biz cards, join professional organizations, meet like-minded women, find a loca-

Hip Tranquil Chick Who's Who

I'm blessed to know some phenom hip and tranquil business chicks. Here are a selection of them offering their words of wisdom.

When I launched my business, I treated it like a challenging sewing project: I visualized the final product, followed the directions carefully, and tweaked it until it was just right.
—**Rachael Ahrens**, chic seamstress

My best advice for anyone teetering on the edge of following that voice inside her heart is simple. Time waits for no one. Do what you love. I discovered my profession long before I had the courage, the confidence, and the guts to take the plunge. I remember one day walking into our local Whole Foods Market and seeing a card that read, "When you leap, you will sprout wings." On the eve of my 29th birthday, I quit my HR job and began teaching yoga full time.

—**Lisa Farmer-Richards**, yoga teacher

When asked about how scary it was to leave a paying job, my answer is always the same: it was scarier for me to be in that mind-numbing, answering-to-a-boss-that-you-can't-stand job than it was to break out on my own.
—**Susan Turnock**, serial entrepreneur

If you want to create your own business, the time is now! If you build it mindfully, and carefully, if you harness all of your resources and gifts, and if you are willing to be flexible and open to change, you can make it happen.
—**Lauren Brownstein**, fundraising and philanthropy consultant

· · · · · · · · · · · · · · · · ·

If you do work that you love, and the work fulfills you, the rest will come.
—Oprah Winfrey

· · · · · · · · · · · · · · · · ·

tion to conduct business, set up trade shows or trunk shows, determine your organizational chart, hire help, place ads, locate your target market, create a mission and vision statement.

Flow: This is where you make it happen. The doors open, your website is launched, your PR campaign is in high gear, you begin to interact with customers and are sure to create a uniquely personalized experience.

Wind down: Slow your flow. Play with ancillary pieces to serve your market—product line, TV show, magazine, blog, speaking podcast. Give back to the community. Regain life balance—sleep, vacation, play, have a day (or two) off, practice more yoga, engage in self-care, enjoy your relationships.

Relaxation: Create a business that can run without you; otherwise you've only created a job.

Let Passion Infuse Your Profession

Doing the necessary Omwork to discover your passion will lead to a more holistic and authentic lifestyle. The path may continue to change, especially as you gain interest in new and exciting worlds. Stay true to your core, notice what motivates you, and strive to explore opportunities that allow you to leave a legacy in some way. For some hip tranquil chicks, it will be through forming their own company, others through starting a family, and still others through working for a cause with which they strongly align. Find work that allows you to lead the lifestyle you crave while also ensuring a passion-filled workday.

. . . .

Your profession is not what
brings home your paycheck.
Your profession is what you
were put on earth to do.
—VIRGIL

. . . .

Omwork

Explore your passions. Make a list of all your passions. Are there ways to turn any of these into a profession? Being able to blend passion into your profession ensures less burnout and puts more spring in your step when heading to the office. Start your day with a passion such as yoga, journal writing, meditation, a swim, a fresh baked croissant, or reading the *Wall Street Journal* and watch the joy infuse your work day.

Take control of your career path. Ask for what you want. Seek out those who can help you move closer toward your ideal profession. Read about inspiring women who have broken through the glass ceiling and made a difference.

Collaborate with other women and fans. Hold a joint trunk or art show. Refer clients to each other. Offer advice and mentor one another. Host special soirées together to share expenses, bring awareness to each other's work, connect with each other's colleagues.

Savvy Sources

Read

Wildly Sophisticated: A Bold New Attitude for Career Success, by Nicole Williams

Second Acts: Creating the Life You Really Want, Building the Career You Truly Desire, by Stephen M. Pollan and Mark Levine

The Girl's Guide to Starting Your Own Business: Candid Advice, Frank Talk, and True Stories for the Successful Entrepreneur, by Caitlin Friedman and Kimberly Yorio

The E-Myth: Why Most Businesses Don't Work and What to Do About It, by Michael Gerber

The Big Sister's Guide to the World of Work: The Inside Rules Every Working Girl Must Know, by Marcelle Langan DiFalco and Jocelyn Greenky Herz

The Girl's Guide to Being a Boss (Without Being a Bitch), by Caitlin Friedman and Kimberly Yorio

Pink Magazine

Visit

www.wildlysophisticated.com
www.ladieswholaunch.com
www.advancingwomen.com
www.woodhull.org

Listen

Brave Faith, by Jana Stanfield

Stan Getz and The Oscar Peterson Trio: The Silver Collection

X & Y, by Coldplay

Mama Said, by Lenny Kravitz

Ray of Light, by Madonna

Chapter 9

Financial Finesse

establish mindful money management

· ·

Wealth is the ability to fully experience life.

—Henry David Thoreau

Financial finesse allows you to have more of a powerful and promising effect on the world. In *The Diamond Cutter*, Michael Roach writes: "There is a belief prevalent in America and other Western countries that being successful, making money, is somehow wrong for people who are trying to lead a spiritual life. In Buddhism, though, it is not the money which is in itself wrong; in fact, a person with greater resources can do much more good in the world than without." Embrace this statement, girls. It's time to take control of your finances and use your money to support a greater good (which may also include the purchase of a new pair of pink Chanel slides).

Embrace being financially self-sufficient and pride yourself on proceeding confidently with an understanding of your over-

all financial profile. When you lack clarity on the big picture, seek assistance from professionals who specialize in financial planning, debt clearing, or tax preparation. Finding a balance between saving for retirement and indulging in a hat-buying fetish is something the hip tranquil chick manages with finesse.

Money Mindset

· ·

We can tell our values by looking
at our checkbook stubs.
—Gloria Steinem

· ·

Our upbringing affects our relationship to money. For example, I recall showing up in Jordache jeans and generic sneakers and feeling a twinge of jealousy at a school where

I was exposed to girls who came from a very different socio-economic status. I avoid debt like the plague, proudly wear signature pieces I find at discount stores, and boldly exclaim, "Oh, thank you, it was only $15 at Tar-*jay*" when complimented. Although I do enjoy indulging in massages or a designer purchase occasionally.

All of our experiences shape us into the exorbitant spender or frugal Fannie we may have become. By taking time to reflect on the following questions, you may uncover some of the emotions behind your own relationship to money.

1. How did you feel growing up about money?
2. Did you earn an allowance? If so, what did you do with the money?
3. Did you pay for your education or postcollege expenses?
4. Are you a saver, spender, or somewhere in between?
5. Was money discussed openly in your family growing up?
6. Did you feel financially in sync with your friends?

Tranquil Tip: Ponder how getting clear on your finances would make your life more tranquil. Let go of fears and start the process today.

Operating from Abundance

A basic premise from the abundance (versus scarcity) mentality is that the more money you make, the more you can assist others. Some of you may not feel comfortable with the notion of acquiring wealth. Maybe you were raised on the biblical notion that it is easier for a camel to fit through the eye of a needle than a rich man to get into heaven, perhaps your parents resented their wealthier siblings, or maybe you have always operated from a scarcity mentality of never having enough. Switching to see the value and ease associated with living an abundant life can have a profound impact on how you treat money.

I have girlfriends who adamantly avoid any discussion of money. It's an uncomfortable and embarrassing topic due to debt, feelings of inadequacy, or simply a lack of knowledge surrounding the topic. As you begin to educate yourself on money and pick up *Kiplinger's* instead of *Us Weekly,* you may be surprised at how fun this topic can become.

Tranquil Tip: Take the time to create systems and a workspace that make it easier for you to manage your money efficiently. Automatic deposits into your checking and savings accounts, online bill payments, and defining a budget are steps toward financial responsibility.

There are people who have money and people who are rich.
—COCO CHANEL

Monitor Your Financial Flow

To truly have financial finesse, it is important to get a grasp on your spending habits. It can be a revelation to see how quickly lunches and happy hours add up, especially coupled with splurges at Sephora and spoiling a newborn niece with all things pink. Once you have an idea of what is coming and going, create a current budget and an ideal budget: one that shows your present state of affairs, and the other that shows an idealized state based on your financial goals.

> Before you can really start setting financial goals, you need to determine where you stand financially.
> —DAVID BACH

Observe the Flow. Begin this analysis by reviewing how much comes in each month. Include your monthly paycheck after taxes, additional income such as bonuses, and other revenue. Estimate one month's spending by categorizing outgoing expenses as *necessities* (such as payments for rent or mortgage, upkeep on a car, gas, utilities, cell phone, insurance, investments, education, food for you and your pet, child care, medical bills), and *luxuries* (such as mani and pedis, espressos, massages, dining out, movies, clothing for you and your pet, accessories, gym memberships, books).

This may seem pretty straightforward, but it will take a good heart-to-heart and a solid weekend of getting intimate with your bank statements, pay stubs, credit card statements, and checkbook from the past year. For an entire week write down every penny that you spend, even that two-dollar energy bar. Review what is left each month. Now designate two separate cards for "necessities" and "luxuries" so you'll have a clearly itemized sheet on where you're allocating your money.

 Tranquil Tip: If you trim just $100 a month starting at the age of 25 and invest it in an account that yields a nominal 4 percent return, you will make $118,590 by the age of 65 and will have only put $48,000 in! If you put $100 a month into an account with a 9 percent return, you'll make $471,643 by the age of 65 and only have been out $48,000! (Source *Smart Women Finish Rich*, by David Bach, page 99.)

Curb Retail-Therapy Debt

I know, it's tough for the modern girl to maintain financial balance with so many temptations, but this is where your *tapas* and *brahmacharya* will come in handy. Maybe you find yourself blowing your annual clothing budget during the postholiday sales in January, or you're a bibliophile who can't say no to the latest Oprah book-club selection. Sure, buying a home or investing in your education will set you back numerous years, but they're more important than that leopard-print stole with pink satin ribbons. Keep in mind the concept of short-term delayed gratification for long-term benefit. A home or education is sure to reap rewards down the

Stretching Your Dollar

If you were shocked by how little is left after all the necessary and not-so-necessary expenses, let's explore simple ideas to do some stretching. There are easy, enjoyable ways to live a bit leaner without feeling deprived.

Old Habit	New Habit	Savings
Buy birthday and holiday gifts	Bake cookies, make soap, or knit legwarmers	$10+ a gift
Shop at trendy boutiques for a special-occasion ensemble	Shop at discount stores that offer designer brands at a great price	$100+ a shopping spree
Buy fresh in-season flowers	Indulge in hearty sunflowers, carnations, bamboo shoots, and potted flowers	$40+ a month
Deck out your condo from the latest chichi furniture boutique	Browse vintage shops and flea markets for great one-of-a kind pieces	$100+ a purchase
Dine out with girlfriends	Join them for drinks and dessert	$100+ a month
Get haircut at trendy salon every six weeks	Wait eight weeks and offer to be a haircut model	$100+ a year
Pay drop-in rates for yoga classes	Buy in bulk when possible and watch your per class price drop	$40+ a month
Buy the latest best-seller or lifesytle pub	Borrow books from the library or buy used. Browse, rather than buy, the latest magazines and books at your big bookstore. If you simply must have magazine subscriptions, share them with a friend.	$30+ a month
Eat out for lunch	Pack your lunch—you'll get exactly what you want and can guarantee nutrition	$200+ a month
See weekly movie with beau	Exchange two movie nights out for in-home renting, complete with popcorn and bubbly water	$40+ a month
Drive to work or cab	Carpool or ride public transportation	$80+ a month
Buy bottled water at corner store	Buy a cute hot pink water bottle and fill it before leaving the house	$40+ a month

road that your stole just can't match. Sorry! If you lose your way, just take a deep breath, rein yourself in, and get back on track.

1. **Pay with cash, a check, or a debit card.** Leave your credit card at home—literally. For emotional shoppers, this is the perfect way to break that habit and avoid accumulating more unworn must-haves with tags still attached. However, if you vow to be more responsible and practice number 5 below, continue using your credit card sparingly and enjoy the accumulation of miles or other bonuses from the generous credit card company.

2. **Consolidate your credit card debt into a low-interest card.** Credit card companies have made it very easy to do this switcheroo, and the time it takes to do the transfer is worth it in the end. Some cards will even offer a no-interest option for a few months. This might allow you to completely get rid of the debt at no additional charge.

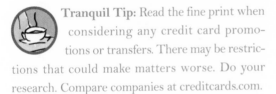

Tranquil Tip: Read the fine print when considering any credit card promotions or transfers. There may be restrictions that could make matters worse. Do your research. Compare companies at creditcards.com.

3. **Never ever use a card that charges an annual fee.** Period. A $25 annual fee adds up to $6,476 at 8 percent interest over 40 years. That is not pocket change—that is a nice down payment on new wheels or your master's degree!

4. **Aggressively begin paying off your credit card debt.** Did you know that if you have a $4,000 balance on a low 5.9 percent interest card and are only paying

$100 a month, it will take you 45 months to pay it off and you will have paid $465 in interest! You will end up paying $2,362 at a typical 18.9 percent interest rate, and it will take you 63 months to pay off $4,000. (Source: *The 9 Steps to Financial Freedom,* by Suze Orman, page 161.) Pay the largest amount you possibly can and ditch this debt. No Prada bag, Gucci eyewear, or Nuala yoga togs are worth this emotional and financial burden. Promise.

5. **Pay off your credit card in full every month.** This is nonnegotiable. If you are going to use your credit card, pay it off monthly. Save time and stress by setting up a system to pay it in full each month automatically. It comes right out of your bank account, so trade an afternoon of writing bills for a tea date with friends.

Tranquil Tip: Organize your financial documents so that you can find everything in a snap. Create files for checking account, taxes, savings account, retirement info, credit card, mortgage/lease, utility bills, investments, and various insurance files. If you put them into brightly colored files and keep them in an organized state, preparing for taxes, meeting with a financial planner, or refinancing your home won't seem so daunting.

Investing in Yourself

Once you're removed your credit card debt, begin setting 5 to 10 percent of your monthly income aside immediately. When you're living paycheck to paycheck with dreams of vacationing along the French Riviera someday, putting money into savings may be the

Investments 101

Hip tranquil chicks, get cozy with your retirement plans, all these acronyms and start saving ASAP. Oh, and one very minor detail: avoid playing with this cash until you've made it to age 59.5 or you may be penalized.

Company 401(k) or nonprofit 403(b): Most plans allow you to contribute up to 15 percent of your salary, capped around $9,500 per year pretax. Some companies also match what you contribute, sometimes up to 100 percent. Huge perk!

IRAs (individual retirement accounts): If you're under the age of 50, you can contribute $4,000 per year to a traditional IRA, tax deductible; withdrawals are subject to tax. Another individual retirement account is the Roth IRA, which also allows you to contribute $4,000 if your adjusted gross income is less than $95,000. Contributions are not tax deductible, but qualified withdrawals are tax and penalty free. You may contribute to both a traditional IRA and a Roth IRA as long as the combined total put into both accounts does not exceed $4,000. SEPs (simplified employment pension plans) and Keogh plans are options for the self-employed.

Diversify your portfolio: Put money into more conservative options such as money market accounts, CDs, bonds, and Treasury bills (T-bills), along with more aggressive mutual funds and stocks. Avoid putting all your eggs in one basket—conservative or aggressive. It is very important to spread your investments into a few baskets to have a truly balanced and abundance-building portfolio.

Seek assistance: Consult a financial adviser to explore your options. Work with a friend or your partner to help each other stay focused on your financial goals.

 Tranquil Tip: Pay yourself first. Put a portion of your earnings automatically into a savings account that earns interest and you won't miss it. The younger you start, the better. At a 12 percent annual interest rate, if you save $2 a day starting at age 20, you will accumulate $1 million by the time you turn 65. However, if you wait until you're age 30, you need to save $6.35 a day, and at age 40, you need to save $20.55 a day to accumulate the same results by 65. This huge difference clarifies the importance of starting now. (Source: *The Wise Investor: Ten Concepts You Need to Know to Achieve Financial Success*, by Neil Elmouchi.)

last thing on your mind. Although I totally understand that mentality, I also know the importance of being short-term savvy for long-term gain. Think about it: the world is constantly changing along with our industries and our best-laid plans. Securing a nest egg of at least three months' living expenses is a modern girl must. This needs to be liquid, available cold hard cash. So start putting that money aside. No ifs, ands, or buts about it. A whole month along the French Riviera can be yours if you save strategically.

Remember the value work we did in chapter 4? Well, your values come into play with your finances too. Hip tranquil chicks seek independence, a comfy lifestyle grounded in consciousness, a sense of freedom, and

. . . .

A big part of financial freedom is having your heart and mind free from worry about the what-ifs of life.

—SUZE ORMAN

. . . .

peace of mind. Review your financial-flow findings and notice if you are aligned with your values. Are you able to balance adventure and freedom with security and peace of mind? If not, what changes can you make to ensure you stay in tune with your values?

 Tranquil Tip: If you're getting antsy to travel, but are low on funds, do a quick day trip to wine country, a nearby beach, or a state park. Pack a picnic. Bring your pals. This is an easy break that is also gentle on the budget. Explore simple, strategic ways that ensure you feel rewarded for your efforts regularly. Little luxuries can go a long way and don't have to break the bank. Let your creativity flow into your finances.

. . . .

What material success does is provide you with the ability to concentrate on other things that really matter. And that is being able to make a difference.

—OPRAH WINFREY

. . . .

Create Financial Fantasies

As you know from chapter 4, it is important to get TRANQUIL about your goals. This same principle applies to your financial goals. Let yourself dream for a moment.

Envision: Financial freedom may include being able to care for an ailing loved one, working from home with your children playing nearby, living in the country, or retiring at 40. Get clear on what constitutes financial freedom to you.

Define: After you've had time to visualize it in your head or pulled images of it from catalogs, put it onto paper. Get clear about what it is that will bring you more in touch with your values while also helping others. Remember that ultimately abundance for you means more for others because you can do a lot more with abundance. Write out your ideal as if it were the present. For example, "I am finishing my novel in a cabin I own in Vail, and living part time in a rented loft in Denver teaching writing classes. I am happy, surrounded by solitude, debt free, and make a comfortable living doing my passion—writing."

Get support: Once you've gotten clear on what financial freedom looks like, share your findings with a trusted companion who will support your dreams. Post your vision where you will see it daily. Carve out weekly reflection time to review your income and expenses, while keeping an eye on the ultimate goal.

Set down small steps that will help lead you to your goal. Rome wasn't built in a day and neither was your ability to feel a strong sense of abundance. Make sure you're removing debt, starting to save, and aligning your finances with your values. Once you take these steps, financial freedom is as close as your own backyard. You control how close and how soon.

Mindful Money Management

Gain control of your financial flow and let your exchange of money be part of your yoga practice. As we know, yoga means "union," and it is necessary to align our financial choices with our values, our desires, and the consciousness of serving a greater good. Reflect on where the money is right now. When you spend your money, where does it go and whom is it serving? Are you shopping for your clothing and gifts at big-box stores or supporting artisan shops and local designers? Observe how and why you spend money. Is it to fulfill a necessity or to soothe an emotion? Recognize your buying patterns. Take steps to create more mindfulness surrounding your exchange of money and watch your practice of yoga off the mat have a positive effect on others.

The exchange of money is a powerful exchange of energy. Do your part to ensure this exchange is done in a way that helps create a more tranquil inner self and outer society.

 Tranquil Tip: Donate anonymously to a charity or person in need without looking for any tax benefit or even gratitude. Think secret Valentine meets good cause. Do it because it feels good. Let this be part of your spiritual practice of giving back.

Easy Education

We take personal growth classes, seminars on professional prosperity, yet rarely set aside time for understanding our financial picture. Empower yourself today by taking these simple steps: Browse the personal investment section of the bookstore. • Set up online banking to help ensure on-time payments and save postage. • Collaborate with a girlfriend and help hold each other accountable to budgets and financial goals. • Take an online or local community college class on basic finances and investing. • Ask for referrals from friends and then interview financial planners to find someone with whom you feel comfortable. • Ask for a gift subscription to a financial magazine—your friends will be impressed! • Seek out socially responsible investments.

Fodder for Financial Finesse

So far we've explored your early experiences with money, your current relationship with greenbacks, several methods to reduce debt, the ways you can invest in yourself, your financial goals, and techniques for a cheap chic lifestyle. Let go of any remaining scarcity thinking. The ability to do good things is not dependent on money, but money does allow you to live more comfortably and more easily assist others along the way. Approach your life practice with a newfound passion for abundance and financial finesse.

Omwork

Reflect on your early experiences with money. How have they shaped you? In what ways do you embrace and resist them? How can you move beyond your early experiences to create your financial fantasy?

Get your finances in order—literally and figuratively. Sort through all your paperwork. Shred items you no longer need. Write out your financial goals. Share them with a symbiotic soul who will support your new financial finesse.

Write out your financial fears and dreams. What holds you back from taking control of your finances? What are you afraid of? Is it lack of will? Why? Is it lack of skill? Search the Internet, browse the bookstore, and get yourself educated. Why wait for Prince Charming when you can be a savvy investor on your own? Face your fears and embrace abundance. You owe it to yourself.

Savvy Sources

Read

The 9 Steps to Financial Freedom: Practical and Spiritual Steps So You Can Stop Worrying, by Suze Orman

The Woman's Book of Money and Spiritual Vision: Putting Your Financial Values into Spiritual Perspective, by Rosemary Williams

Smart Women Finish Rich: 9 Steps to Achieving Financial Security and Funding Your Dreams, by David Bach

The Diamond Cutter: The Buddha on Managing Your Business and Your Life, by Geshe Michael Roach

City Chic: An Urban Girl's Guide to Livin' Large on Less, by Nina Willdorf

Smart Money magazine

Kiplinger's magazine

Visit

www.fool.com

www.finishrich.com

www.suzeorman.com

www.myfico.com

www.lowermybills.com

Listen

The Eminem Show, by Eminem

Aznavour: Ses Plus Grands Succès, by Charles Aznavour

Bunkka, by Paul Oakenfold

Prose Combat, by MC Solaar

Asia Lounge: Asian Flavoured Club Tunes– Third Floor, by various artists

Delete the negative;

accentuate the positive!

—DONNA KARAN

Combo Chic

Combo chic is where the inner and
outer chic combine to create a
truly luxurious and tranquility-filled
modern girl. By infusing your style,
surroundings, and global mindset
with the precepts of yoga, your entire
lifestyle will flow and exude that
postpractice glow.

Chapter 10

Signature Style

clothing and accessory must-haves for the yogini

Fashion is not something that exists in dresses only.

Fashion is in the sky, in the street, fashion has to do

with ideas, the way we live, what is happening.

—Coco Chanel

A signature style is a way to flaunt your personality through your lifestyle. A hip tranquil chick loves showing her internal world through her clothing and accessories. Sharing your signature style is a creative form of self-expression that makes your friends exclaim, "Oh, this is so her!" when finding the perfect thing for you.

Hip and tranquil fashionistas know how to turn yoga-practice outfits into a dinner or dancing delight with the right accessories, wrap top, and fun shoes. Create a personal style that helps you stand out from the crowd, and make versatility your middle name. Embrace your inner artist and express it through your style.

Weed Out Your Wardrobe

In order to exude your savvy signature style, you must first determine what you have. It's never an easy task if you aren't the most organized fashionista, but there are simple ways to start the assessment. Have a girlfriend on hand, as she won't have the emotional connection to that fuchsia unitard that you do. Then begin by pulling everything you have out of your closet.

To be aware is more important
than what you wear.
—Kenneth Cole

Follow the old rule: if you haven't worn it in over a year, let it go, girl. Practice the art of detachment and surrender this beloved piece to someone who will actually wear it! Then separate what's left of your loot into four piles:

1. Pieces you can throw on any day of the week and feel fabulous (keepers)
2. Pieces in good shape, but you're over them (donate to charity)
3. Pieces to send to clothing heaven (stained, torn beyond repair, or too worn)
4. Pieces that need some TLC (repair, alterations, cleaning)

Categorize your closet into on-the-town wear (little black dress, sassy skirts, leather pants); on-the-mat wear (rollover black pants, fitted tops, wraparound sweaters); casual hang-at-home wear (pajamas, terry and velour suits); office and professional wear (suits, crisp white shirts); jeans; and special-occasion wear (dresses for weddings or holiday wear). Once you have them categorized, colorize them.

Put less commonly worn pieces such as skiwear and beachwear in a labeled bin on a top shelf (unless you live on a beach or at a ski resort). Move out-of-season pieces like heavy coats and boots away from your skimpy summer wear. Fewer choices will feel less daunting when engaging your artistic flair. Keep your daily wear handy and at the forefront of your closet.

 Tranquil Tip: To weave in the yogic principle of *tapas*, make it a habit to give away at least one item for every new piece you add to your closet. This will help keep your wardrobe from growing too large with tons of last year's must-haves. Also, determine at the beginning of fall and spring what new pieces you need to update your wardrobe, and write these down. Avoid on-the-fly shopping and coming home with emotional pieces that will sit for months in your closet with the tags on.

Boutique Beauty

When reorganizing your closet, think of it as a tiny swank boutique—a special housing of your personal signature style. Tape up images on the inside of your closet doors with captivating outfits you've craved in magazines. Explore ways to play with your look by putting together some of what you already have on hand. The more organized and stylish your closet feels, the more fun you'll have creating your masterpiece look. If you need new pieces to complete the look, keep a wish list based on the missing staples or must-haves inside your closet door. This will help you stay focused when engaging in the fine art of retail shopping as you can have our list in tow.

Top 10 Staples for the Hip Tranquil Chick's Closet

A hip tranquil chick blends style with comfort and versatility, so it is imperative that your closet be chock-full of pieces that offer both—even your favorite dark denim jeans. The girl-on-the-go's closet should have:

1. Multiple black pants in assorted fabrics (velvet, terry, organic cotton blends, bamboo, velour) and assorted styles (palazza, leggings, floor-length flare, low-rise capri, gaucho, drawstring, dress).

2. Fitted, flattering tees. A stack of fresh white and black tanks are a must, but here's where you can also add a dash of color and layers to the all-black look.

3. A black cashmere ballet wrap, cardigan, or V-neck sweater. Perfect for layering.

4. A chemise-style dress or sassy strapless tube tunic to be worn over yoga pants or jeans, and alone as the perfect LBD (little black dress).

5. Black slip-on kitten heels, ballet flats, and tall wedge boots are comfy yet funky enough for wearing to the studio and then to a date at the corner café. Wear bulky white tennis shoes only if you're running! Slim hot pink Pumas are my choice for blending function and fashion when walking the hilly streets of San Francisco or trekking through a favorite fern-lined path in Muir Woods.

6. A great tote bag, large enough to hold all your goodies in hip and practical fashion, and not look schlumpy. My greatest find was the Marc Jacobs Stella bag. Holds everything, including my iBook, planner pad, and latest novel!

7. Multiple black skirts: asymmetrical, below the knee, mini, ankle length, fitted, flared.

8. Jacket that matches a skirt. Wear with your skirt as a suit or solo with jeans and heels.

9. Two pairs of dark denim jeans: a longer pair to wear with heels and a shorter pair to wear with black patent leather ballet flats.

10. A coat that screams you: leopard, camel suede with lamb's wool, petal pink trench.

Let Your Style Flow with Creativity

How we present ourselves to the world says a lot about who we are and how we'll be perceived. Perhaps you wear navy suits when your soul longs for bold colors, or you find your closet to be a mini-Talbots while you prefer the funky style of Betsey Johnson. If this is you, adding a dash of creativity to your style can do wonders for your overall look.

> In order to be irreplaceable one must always be different.
> —Coco Chanel

Take the time to creatively explore your personal style and be prepared for amazing effects on how you feel about yourself. A girlfriend once told me that she viewed putting on her makeup as art. Mixing the brushes with various shades of eye shadows were her way of showcasing her artistic side with the world every day. How can you let your inner artist shine as you get ready each morning? Don't be afraid to play. Dressing isn't serious. Mix it up.

Adornment is never anything except a reflection of the heart.
—Coco Chanel

Build Style with Savvy

The easiest and most economical way to update your wardrobe is through accessories. Adding a simple scarf or multicolored beaded necklace can make even the most overworn white T-shirt-and-jeans combo shine. Indulge in high-quality staples such as a great coat, a delightful designer handbag, shoes that will survive several seasons, a great pair of sunglasses, and the perfect hip-hugging jeans. By buying all your basic staples at reasonable outlets, you will be able to indulge each season in at least one classic high-quality piece to add longevity to your wardrobe.

I have heard with admiring submission the experience of the lady who declared that the sense of being perfectly well dressed gives a feeling of inward tranquility which religion is powerless to bestow.
—Ralph Waldo Emerson

Bring More Flair into Everyday Wear
Play with your hairstyle. • Twirl your hair and pin it with bobby pins. • Wrap a scarf into your hair, around your waist or wrist, or tie onto your handbag. • Wear a skirt over your yoga pants. • Add a splash of color to your basic blacks. • Wear a silver sequined belt over your yoga togs. • Carry a brown and blue toile umbrella. • Wear Pucci-inspired goulashes to brighten up rainy days. • Shop a vintage, thrift, or resale store for a unique find. • Find leopard-print stilettos that make you feel sexy. • Wear long faux pearls with your basic white tee and dark denim jeans.

5 Perfect Mat-to-Night-Out Ensembles

Running between yoga classes, meetings, errands, and dates means wearing pieces that can transition easily in all these varied situations. For those of us with a limited wardrobe and budget, here are five perfect outfits based on staple yoga wear.

Build with the basics: black capri leggings and a fitted cami with shelf bra in any color.

Spice up this fundamental yoga look: (1) tall boots, a colorful wrap dress, and bangle bracelets; (2) flip-flops, a basic white tee, and a mid-length black skirt that allows the leggings to peek out below; (3) leopard-print ballet flats, long black tunic that covers the bum, and a long, pink, skinny scarf to throw around your neck; (4) black sequined slip-

ons, strapless tube dress, and headscarf; (5)
kitten heels, silk chemise slip dress, and big
chandelier earrings. Voilà! You're ready to
transition from the mat onto the town without losing the comfy leggings and cami in
which you practiced down dog.

Add flair: Tie a scarf
around your hips, slip on
a sequined headband,
pull on arm or leg
warmers, add a skirt
or wrap top over
your basic yoga
gear to fancy it up
while on the mat.
Your yoga mat is
a sacred place, so
be sure to let your
inner goddess shine
in what you wear
when practicing!

Add "Oms" (a.k.a. Accessorizing)

Sure, hand-knit fluffy leg warmers can add
oomph to your all-black look, but we cannot overlook the importance of attitude. My
number one recommendation for accessorizing is to don that smile—even when interacting with in-laws. This will get you further
than you'll ever know both personally and
professionally.

All in all, accessorizing is a skill that can
be honed with practice. Figure out what
your favorite accessories are. These will
become part of your signature style. Try big
sunglasses, chunky layered necklaces, boots
year-round, retro buttons or brooches on
jackets, dangly rhinestone earrings, big belts
over everything, or an oversized sparkly dinner ring.

Whatever your overall passion for accessories, let yourself have fun with the experience.
Even if you're on a budget, a well-acces-
sorized look can do so much to add panache
to your wardrobe. And remember to never
leave home without your smile and fun-loving
attitude.

Inner and Outer Flair

A signature style is the full package—attitude, clothing, makeup, hair, and skin. In
order to stay put together, it is important
to choose products that match your style,
specialized needs, and budget. Practice
ahimsa and avoid products tested on animals
or harmful to the environment.

Manis and pedis: Let us not forget the hip tranquil chick's nails! Pedis are an absolute must for showing off a passion for self-care in yoga class. A French pedi goes with every-thing and lasts for weeks. Now, manis are a bit challenging for hip tranquil chicks who have their hands in the soil while gardening, clay while creating pottery, or yoga mat while practicing jump-backs. Do simple upkeep on your own by shaping nails into a square and topping them off with a nude polish. This keeps them happy and healthy without tak-ing much time from your busy schedule.

Face and body know-how: Pare facial care down to four essentials and save pre-cious time (and money): a gentle cleanser like Cetaphil, a light and refreshing rosewater toner, a daytime moisturizer with sunscreen, and a heavy evening moisturizer. Try an all-in-one product like Organic Essential, which offers hair and body wash in one handy bot-tle to avoid all the fuss.

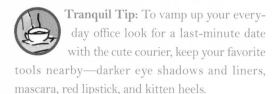

Tranquil Tip: To vamp up your every-day office look for a last-minute date with the cute courier, keep your favorite tools nearby—darker eye shadows and liners, mascara, red lipstick, and kitten heels.

On the top: Taking good care of your hair is crucial to topping off your signature style. Get regular haircuts. Nourish your hair with various masks and deep conditioners and envision your hair smiling with glee. If you prefer having your hair out of your face, pull it back with a funky headband instead of a slick ponytail that may cause breakage. Or try putting your hair up in a mini-bun by pull-ing it back loosely into a ponytail and gently wrapping the band around the folded-over

ponytail. This look is light, and the hair has less chance for breakage. Couple this with sparkly barrettes to keep bangs out of the face during down dog, or a Pucci print heads-carf, and you've got a chic look for a not-so-fabulous hair or an exhausting travel day.

Tranquil Tip: Many places now offer the opportunity to create your very own scent. Whether you are a citrus gal or want something more floral, find a signature scent that will whisper your presence as you sweep through any room. Personally I am addictted to The Body Shop's white musk perfume oil.

Inner care: Don't forget your multivitamin. This little gem can help keep your internal and external systems happy. Keep Emergen-C packets on hand, too. Just add the powder to water, and you've got tons of vitamin C and other goodies infusing your system.

Quintessential Hip Chick Ritual

If you wear concealer, search for a **tinted moisturizer** that feeds your thirsty skin while also covering blemishes. Think win-win! There are also fabulously tingly **lip moisturizers** with color (Burt's Bees Merlot lip shimmer is a 5-star). Since you're constantly on the go, there is no time for drips—buy **waterproof mascara** and douse your upper lids. Keep some **powder sheets** on hand as a fun way to dab off an excessive yoga glow. **Eyeliner** across the upper lid can help those doe eyes pop! Never forget the power of **tidy brows**—a nice waxing helps frame your eyes beautifully. Ah, never fear, the price is not too high: $10–$20 and well worth it.

Hip Tranquil Travel

So you've decided to jetset for a weekend or weeklong escapade, below are some little treats for your suitcase to make your travel more tranquil while maintaining your signature style.

Basics: Nothing is worse than slipping on a carpet during down dog. Take a **yoga mat** for your hotel-room practice. **Scented candles—** I like lavender or lilac—are wonderful for the bathroom. Look for the ones in small tins for easy transport, and don't forget matches! **Noise-reducing headphones** or earplugs are a huge help on the plane. **Journal.** Plenty of **pens** to record your thoughts. Don't forget some **gum** to help relieve any postflight ear pressure, and **aspirin** to help recover from a red-eye.

Self-care: Bring some of your favorite herbal **tea bags** for hotels who think Earl Grey is the only tea. **Healthy snacks** like almonds, nutrition bars, and plenty of water. **Bath treats. Rosebud salve** reduces hair frizzies, soothes lips, relieves dry skin, and smells divine. **A silk eye pillow** soothes tired, jet-lagged eyes. Moist **body and face wipes** are a great pick-me-up for the weary traveler.

Entertainment: Go through your **magazines** on the plane and bring at least two powerful books to motivate and inspire. How did we ever survive before we could carry around our entire CD collection in one tiny **iPod**? Digital **camera.**

Togs: Pack wrinkle-free, comfy clothing. Think flattering, color-coordinated, and trendy separates. Take your favorite pair of **jeans,** comfy **slip-ons** that ensure style during long treks, and a **swimsuit.** (Don't you always find that the hotel has a pool or a hot tub your tired body craves but you forgot the suit?) Don't forget a **little black dress:** throw on kitten heels to dress it up to hit a posh café or your slip-ons and a denim jacket for exploring the sights. And, of course, a few of your **flair-filled accessories** to transform your basic clothing pieces into extravagant ensembles.

Savvy Sleeping Secrets

You've probably realized how essential a good night's sleep is to your overall well-being. There is a direct correlation between sleeping well and feeling great. Here are a few of my favorite tips for savvy sleeping.

1. **Invest in a few pairs of earplugs.** Sleeping with a pug that snores incessantly has forced me to invest in the best earplugs I could find. If they fall out during your tossing and turning, have extras nearby to ensure you don't loose any precious shut-eye time.

2. **Indulge in a silk lavender-scented eye pillow.** Nothing soothes more than the

feeling of cool silk on tired eyes when you first crawl into bed.

3. **Put on a soothing CD.** Ah, the joys of falling asleep to the sounds of the ocean or a thunderstorm. Have these tunes playing as you drift off to sleep, or programmed as a more peaceful wake-up call in the morning than a loud buzz.

4. **Drink plenty of water.** Have your handy replenisher nearby so that you don't have to stumble into the kitchen half-awake to quench your thirst.

5. **Spray the pillow.** Spritzing on a little chamomile, rose, or lavender is sure to help you dream in peace.

6. **Apply lip gloss.** Yep, can't do anything without gloss on these lips—that includes sleep. I have a tub of various heavy-duty clear glosses on my bedstand. Aveeno Intense Relief has become my tub 'o choice.

Signature Style 101

It's true: others will form their first impression of you within a few seconds. By taking an active role in the image you project, you exude your most fabulous self while staying true to who you are. To ensure your signature style comes from a place of authenticity, stay mindful of how you walk into a room, observe how you conduct yourself in meetings and interviews, ensure you live passionately in your daily life, and let it flow on the yoga mat.

Embodying a style that projects your personality is sure to have a positive effect on how you feel about yourself, and how others perceive you. Build on your assets by emphasizing your uniqueness. You may be six feet tall and in love with stilettos or platinum blonde and wear all white. Let these unique styles share a story with others about who you are. Celebrate your differences. Enjoy what makes you unique. Play it up, and revel in your own personal style.

Omwork

Collect images that appeal to you from various magazines and put together a style collage to post inside your closet door. Are the images trendy, or more classic? Bold colors and styles, or subdued and timeless? Channel your favorite style icon. Is it Jackie O or Gwen Stefani?

Invest in accessories that can wow even the most basic black leggings and white tee. Find special pieces that you treasure. Shop discount specialty stores to pick up the trendy must-haves. Peruse vintage or second-hand shops for more unique trinkets.

Weed out your wardrobe. Clothing, shoes, or accessories that have not been worn in over a year (excluding special-occasion gear) should be donated to a local women's shelter or offered up during a girl's-night-in swap.

Savvy Sources

Read

The Pocket Stylist: Behind-the-Scenes Expertise from a Fashion Pro on Creating Your Own Look, by Kendall Farr

Style, by Kate Spade

What Not to Wear for Every Occasion, by Trinny Woodall and Susannah Constantine

Daily Candy A to Z: An Insider's Guide to the Sweet Life, by the editors of DailyCandy

Daring to Be Yourself, by Alexandra Stoddard

Entre Nous: A Woman's Guide to Finding Her Inner French Girl, by Debra Ollivier

Retail Therapy: Life Lessons Learned While Shopping, by Amanda Ford

Visit

www.shefinds.com
www.budgetfashionista.com
www.girlshop.com
www.tranquiliT.com
www.dailycandy.com
www.ebay.com

Listen

Una Leyenda Flamenca, by Camarón de la Isla

Café Ibiza, by various artists

Careless Love, by Madeleine Peyroux

Harry on Broadway: Act I, by Harry Connick Jr.

Ministry of Sound: Chillout Sessions, by various artists

Asana 3, by various artists

Best of Blondie, by Blondie

Chapter 11

Soulful Surroundings

design an oasis at home and work

· ·

Surround yourself with people, color,

sounds and work that nourish you.

—SARK

Let your surroundings reflect your unique character and exotic personality—all pieces of your signature style. Your environment directly affects your relationship to yourself and others. Taking the time to create an environment that nurtures your soul may help other areas of your life fall into place. Even if you share a city apartment with a group of girls, or have a suburban home with five kids, you can find simple ways to sprinkle tranquility into your home and work life.

Let's explore ways to find inspiration and a mini-retreat in your surroundings. Your home can be a comfortable and inviting space that serves as a respite from the world, along with a place to entertain and host savvy soirées. Project to the world a glimpse into your soul when others step into your sacred space.

Thrive in your oasis, and create it with intention and passion—two oh-so-important traits of the hip tranquil chick.

Create Order and Declutter

The creation of soulful surroundings starts with assessing what you have, along with what you can, and can't, live without. Look around your home. Maybe you observe a sense of chaos, piles of half-written Post-It notes, heaps of unopened mail, and various tea mugs on your desk. Just as you weeded through your wardrobe, so you will find it helpful to do the same thing with the armoire, bookshelves, linen closet, catch-all drawers, bathroom pantry, desk drawers, and kitchen cupboards. Pull everything out and assess its state—but do one area at a time. If you try to overhaul a full house, you'll end up exhausted and disillusioned. Do this while watching a favorite movie or listening to a great new CD. Make it fun!

Start small and gather the tools needed. For example, when going through a desk armoire, make sure to have a trash can, shredder, file folders, and a felt-tip pen nearby to organize the materials. When going through a bathroom pantry, have a designated donation bag, washcloth, and cleaning supplies on hand to clean up any spilled products. Discard all outdated products.

 Tranquil Tip: Cover a shoebox with decorative wrapping paper or wallpaper to hold photos, mementos, note cards, desk paraphernalia, sewing tools, ribbons, and gift bags. They stack nicely and can be wrapped in coordinating prints to match your style (toile, floral, polka dot, leopard).

The mental energy and space that you get from organizing can have a profound effect—actually making you feel lighter. We collect clutter every day simply by bringing in mail, a new magazine, business cards from a meeting, or the daily paper. Get in the habit of dealing with it immediately (filing it away, putting data into your Palm, throwing papers away) or setting aside certain pieces such as magazines in a designated spot (pending clutter basket) to skim when you have blocks of time—in the bathtub, on a plane, or a lazy Sunday afternoon.

Embrace the yogic principle of *saucha* and keep your home and its belongings clutter free and simple. Get in the habit of ensuring that everything has a place and asking yourself whether you really need something before making a purchase. Nothing will help you break the hoarding mentality quite like moving. You'll soon realize that you don't really need all the items you've accumulated. Let them go—I promise you'll breathe better.

 Tranquil Tip: Make decluttering into an event: have a cup of tea nearby and nostalgic music playing. It's fun to go through old letters, cards, and photos. Categorize the pieces into years (1999–2001) or events (college or European trip). Toss all that stuff that no longer has meaning. Be relentless.

Set Your Soulful Style

Now that you have released yourself of clutter, it's time to determine your design. Is it chic and sassy, complete with leopard print, pink accents, and chandeliers? Is it romantic

Louis the Tranquility-Invoking Pug.

 Having a pet to love and cuddle can bring joy on so many levels. My baby Louis has infused my home with such soul. From his desire to be loved at all times to his knowledge of certain words that we now have to spell (T-R-E-A-T), I have found his presence to be incredibly cathartic and uplifting. Despite his use of my iBook as a chew toy, his playful nature truly adds to an atmosphere of tranquility.

Habitat Must-Haves

Terah Kathryn Collins, the founder of the Western School of Feng Shui, says, "Every second our nervous systems are responding to our surroundings, whether we are conscious of it or not." Be sensitive to how your body responds to the sights, sounds, and smells around you. Beginning with the suggestions here, find a balance between calming your senses and pumping them up.

Smell: Oodles of organic scented soy candles. Fresh flowers like tuberoses from the corner flower stand. Incense or a sage smudge stick. Linen sprays. Lavender sachets for your closets, drawers, or tied to your door handles. A freshly baked pie. Scented bath products. Aromatherapy lamps. Fresh laundry.

Sight: Lots of live greenery—easy-to-care-for plants such as philodendron and lucky bamboo. Splashes of color through flowers, pillows, paint, and draped fabrics to spice up a monochromatic space. Sunshine. Pictures of loved ones or artwork strategically displayed. Framed postcards of all the places you've been and loved. Mirrors to give the illusion of more space.

Touch: Faux fur, silks, Egyptian cotton and other divine fabrics. Chenille throws. Sisal rugs. Velvet, organza, or beaded curtains. Smooth stone sculptures. A pet to nurture—goldfish count, too!

Sound: Delicate wind chimes outside the bedroom window. The nurturing sounds of drawing a bath. A crackling fire. Classical, jazz, or soothing music. Water sculpture or fountain. Early-morning sounds from an open window. Birds singing.

Taste: Fresh fruit in a wicker basket or ceramic bowl. A display of teas and hot chocolate on your kitchen counter. Clear Mason jars filled with nuts and grains. Red wine. A candy dish. Fresh lemonade with floating rasberries in a crystal pitcher.

---

shabby chic, filled with florals, white-washed furniture, and wicker? Is it minimalist Zen girl spaciously decorated with bamboo floors, sisal rugs, and only the bare essential furniture? Beginning with a clear vision of the vibe is key.

Put together a storyboard where you keep swatches of fabrics and color cards, along with images from magazines that resonate with your look before you begin making purchases. By putting all of the pieces together in a physical manifestation before buying, you can see how the hot pink settee doesn't quite go with the Zen-esque look you were hoping for. Taking the time to do your research and homework upfront ensures a cohesive and cozy environment.

Design on a Budget

Nothing enhances a room and is as easy on the purse strings as color. When I moved into my first condo, I splashed the living area walls with raspberry pink. Yes, it was bold and a far cry from all the rented white-walled apartments I'd had over the years, but the color really makes a statement and broadcasts sassy femininity.

By thinking outside the box, perusing Pottery Barn or the crafts section of a bookstore for ideas, and taking time to check out alternatives, you can easily create a dreamy, cozy home that embodies your signature style. The ability to pull a look together for a home—as it does for a closet—comes from touches such as zebra-print pillows, chandeliers, super-soft bedding, white-washed frames, water fountains, crown molding, lots of greenery, and fresh flowers. Your retreat is only a few fabulous accessories away.

A $500 Makeover

Here is how I transformed my first 400-square-foot studio into my very own haven: I got my couch and sitting chairs at second-hand stores. A slipcover and some good cleaning later, I had a comfy set without making much of a dent in my budget. For a coffee

> It's not houses I love,
> it's the life I live in them.
> —COCO CHANEL

ing much of a dent in my budget. For a coffee table, I used a darling white wood stool bench purchased at a discount store. My first dining room set was natural wood that I painted white. I added floral fabric to the plain seat cushions with a staple gun and screwdriver. To top it off, with my limited sewing skills, I

made curtains and a tablecloth to match the ensemble. Finally, my four-post canopy bed (something I'd dreamed of as a little girl) came from a mattress discount store and was yet another bargain. I also sewed a lovely matching swag to drape along the canopy. Throw in some signature accessories, and voilà! A cheap and chic castle was born.

Let's Go Green, Girlfriend

We all know plants are a fabulous addition to any home. They provide oxygen while absorbing our carbon dioxide, and according to research by the Flower Council, they absorb noise and reduce headaches. You

Infuse Your Crib with Creativity

Cook with a new herb, spice, or sauce and let the aroma fill your home. • Create an inspiration nook complete with a meditation cushion, framed art postcards, candles, inspiring books, and a pot of tea. • String white Christmas lights along your fence, balcony, or trees. • Eat dinner by candlelight while Sinatra serenades in the background. • Stack art books on your coffee table as a reminder to nurture your creative side. • Create a festive home spa in your bathroom filled with colorful bath soaps, salts, confetti, and candles. • Add a leopard-print duvet cover and tons of fluffy pink pillows to your bed. • Make an indoor Zen garden with sand and rocks.

Home Spa, Baby

Turn your home into a sacred spa and watch for cleansing effects on your well-being.

Step 1. Begin by carving out at least an hour. Run the perfect-temperature bath water, and add drops of chamomile and lavender essential oil along with fresh rose petals. Add your favorite products, light a candle, and have bubbly water to sip nearby.

Step 2. While the water fills, do a rosewater facial steam with 1 cup fresh rose petals and 1 gallon almost-boiling water. Put petals into a bowl, add water, and cover your head with a towel as you lean over the bowl. Keep your face 10 to 12 inches from the bowl and steam for 10 to 15 minutes.

Step 3. Next, hop into the tub with a pineapple facial mask applied: one 1-inch slice of pineapple with the skin on, cut into chunks and blend with 3 tablespoons olive oil until almost smooth. Apply to face, and leave on for 10 to 15 minutes. Rinse face with warm water and pat dry. Spritz face with rosewater atomizer while soaking.

Step 4. Practice your three-part yogic breath. Close your eyes and listen to the flickering of the candle. Let go into your very own home spa.

---

may have a ton of space to create a garden, but even a fire escape can serve as a haven for your special green babies. Tie up window boxes to a railing, plant impatiens, and hang a basket of petunias off the fire escape. These little gems will keep you happy and connected to life, plus add color for almost six months out of the year. You can also plant an herbal tea garden or a bath and body garden with plants such as mint, lavender, aloe, rosemary, lemongrass, lemon verbena, and rose hips. Don't let a lack of outdoor space keep you from getting in touch with your green thumb. You're bound to have a window somewhere and can make use of it in creative ways. Debra Ollivier, author of *Entre Nous: A*

Woman's Guide to Finding Her Inner French Girl, writes that "For the French girl, the garden is a microcosm of the world, a wild open space where the cycles of nature play out under her fingertips, bringing her persistent small pleasures on a daily basis." Go ahead girls, get those hands dirty. *Si vous plaît.*

A Beautiful Boudoir

Your bedroom should serve as the ultimate retreat every time you step into it. If you work from home and live in a studio or one-bedroom apartment, this can be a challenge. However, I encourage you to ensure tranquility in this very special room. It is best to forgo a TV, computer, or exercise equipment in your boudoir. If you have a home office, keep your laptop and work paraphernalia in a different area of the house, or in an armoire or desk that closes when not in use.

One-third of our lives are spent in our bed! That's a lot of hours over the course of a lifetime. Make sure they are luxuriously and comfortably spent. Keep all the tranquil tools mentioned in chapter 10's savvy sleeping secrets near your bedside. Be sure to include a pad of paper and pen for those "Aha!" moments that arise throughout various states of slumber.

 Tranquil Tip: Think of your bedding as a wardrobe for your boudoir. Avoid scrimping on your sheet sets (high thread count Egyptian organic cotton or lush bamboo sheets are fabulous finds), locate the perfect duvet, and invest in an assortment of pillows—thin, thicker, goose down, poly—to vary with your moods and placement needs.

Workspace Wonders

Our workspace can serve to inspire or disempower. Even if it isn't clear how you could possibly find serenity in accounting, law, or admin work, there are ways to create tranquil surroundings that will feed your productivity and creativity. If you find that approaching your desk, office, or workspace fills you with a sense of dread, it is time to make some tiny changes. Since so many of your waking hours may be filled with work, infuse your personality into your environment and improve your attitude toward it.

Girl-on-the-Go Vinyasa

Connecting within is crucial to creating soulful surroundings—for you and those who cross your path throughout your day. For a 15-minute "mental-health break," infuse this sequence into your daily on-the-go routine. Begin by sitting on the edge of your seat with feet hip-width apart and flat on the ground.

Tranquility at Work

It's the little things that will keep you sane. • Slippers hidden under your desk offer great respite from your stilettos. • Have a cozy cashmere wrap nearby to help keep you warm during those over-air-conditioned days. • Lamps create a lovely ambience separate from the yucky fluorescent lighting. • Have a pink down throw strewn across the extra chair in your office—perfect for those spontaneous picnics in the park, or to cover your legs on a chilly day. • Create a comfort drawer complete with personal care products—moisturizer, lip gloss, facial cleaning pads, mascara, tampons, headache control, white musk perfume oil, lavender aromatherapy oil, and green tea. • Write your company mission, organizational values, or monthly sales projections on colorful note cards to hang on a polka dot ribbon from your corkboard or wall. • Have a lavender-scented candle nearby—ready to be lit at deadline notice.

Extend the crown of the head toward the ceiling to create an elongated spine. Connect to your breath.

1. **Neck and shoulder rolls with closed eyes.** Close the eyes. Inhale and lengthen the spine and lower your right ear to your right shoulder. Exhale and lower the chin to the chest. Inhale and move the left ear to the left shoulder. Exhale and lower the chin to the chest. Repeat 5 times. Inhale and roll the shoulders forward and up to your ears. Exhale and roll the shoulders back and down your back. Repeat 5 times in both directions.

2. **Seated cat and cow.** Clasp the seat of the chair with your fingers pointing toward the floor. Inhale, lift the heart center, and draw the shoulder blades together. Take a slight back bend into cow pose. Exhale, bring your belly toward the back of the chair, and lower the shoulders forward into cat pose. Repeat 5 to 10 times.

3. **Chair twists.** Inhale and cross your right leg over your left. Exhale and place the left hand on your right knee, and your right hand on the back of your chair. Inhale; lengthen. Exhale; twist. Let your head follow the twist of the spine. Gaze over your right shoulder. Remain here with your breath for 30 seconds to 1 minute. Inhale and return to the center. Repeat on the other side.

4. **Eagle arms.** Inhale and stretch the arms out to the sides. Exhale and bring your left arm under your right arm. Cross both arms at the elbows; point the elbows toward the floor and fingers upward. Try to place the palms of the hands together with both arms externally rotated. Inhale and raise your elbows to shoulder height. Exhale and draw circles with the elbows in one direction and then the other. Repeat on the other side.

5. **Seated pigeon pose with fold.** Inhale and place your right ankle on your left knee. Exhale and fold forward. Place your hands or forearms on your thighs, or let them dangle to the floor as you lower your chest to your thighs. Hold for 1 minute. Repeat on other side.

6. **Walking meditation.** As you walk to the copier or to refill your water bottle during the workday, bring awareness to each step and arm movement. Feel your feet connect to the earth. Notice sensations in your body, concentrate on your breath, and practice awareness of your surroundings. Bring mindfulness into the mundane.

Surroundings Gone Soulful

Your environment can help keep your spirits high or unhinge you when in disarray. As stated by decorator extraordinaire Alexandra Stoddard in *Creating a Beautiful Home,* "Houses speak your language. Rooms take on your sensitivity, mood, attitude, and spirit. And when you are feeling discouraged, your four walls will comfort you because they will reflect back on you, remind you of your energy and personality. A house becomes your friend; the furniture, your possessions, your most intimate circle."

Take the time to make your surroundings reflect your spirited personality. A hip tranquil chick needs to refuel in the oasis she calls home and office. By infusing your environment with these simple tips, you'll have the energy to shine when it matters most—because you've been able to fill your well in a surrounding that nurtures your soul.

Omwork

Organizational overhaul. Once you've begun creating comfort at home and in your office, keep the momentum up. Have a designated place for all those miscellaneous must-haves that wreak havoc on categorization. Label drawers, catch-all tins, shelves, boxes, files, and closets until you get in the habit of putting your pieces in their proper home.

Ensure order in your home or office by drawing up a list of five new habits you'd like to create. One simple habit may be stopping work 10 minutes early to clear your workspace. Another may be promising never to exit your car with trash inside. Take extra care to get your personal space in order by doing these small steps one at a time. Enjoy the freedom that comes along with thwarting the disorder before it gets out of hand.

Practice feng shui. Incorporate the five elements of nature into your surroundings—wood, fire, earth, metal, and water. Adding pieces such as a ficus tree, lamp, soft sisal rug and earthtone pillows, silver picture frame with a family photo, fish tank, and fountains can help you connect to these natural elements while inside your sacred space.

Savvy Sources

Read

Office Spa: Stress Relief for the Working Week, by Darrin Zeer

You Grow Girl: The Groundbreaking Guide to Gardening, by Gayla Trail

Creating a Beautiful Home, by Alexandra Stoddard

Moving On: Creating Your House of Belonging with Simple Abundance, by Sarah Ban Breathnach

Visit

www.traceyporter.com

www.shabbychic.com

www.alexandrastoddard.com

Listen

The Very Best of Marvin Gaye, by Marvin Gaye

Stevie Wonder: The Definitive Collection, by Stevie Wonder

The Road to Ensenada, by Lyle Lovett

Rogamar, by Cesária Évora

Keep on Moving: The Best of Angélique Kidjo, by Angélique Kidjo

Sinatra Reprise: The Very Good Years, by Frank Sinatra

Chapter 12

Savvy Social Consciousness

expand your global mindset

· ·

Everyone thinks of changing the world,

but no one thinks of changing himself.

—LEO TOLSTOY

Some women have confessed to me that they struggle to do the right thing when making everyday choices. To buy organic or not? To buy American made or not? To buy from a big box store or an indie boutique with higher prices? Sometimes you may not make the perfect decision; sometimes others may feel it wasn't the most conscious. However, we all have our reasons for a certain purchase or action and when done mindfully with intention, we hope to have a positive effect overall.

All of the ideas presented throughout this chapter are suggestions for becoming more socially conscious. Consumerism is a huge part of this. Price is important to us all, but keep in mind that with every purchase you are "voting" and supporting a business, stating what you believe is important. What do your purchases say about your values?

Remember to approach these ideas with balance and moderation, *brahmacharya*. A hip tranquil chick does her best even if she has a penchant for designer handbags. She can still practice consciousness by the products she puts inside.

Vive la Revolution!

Connect to the passions that drive you. Maybe you have experienced an unhealthy relationship and want to assist others in escaping in the same cycle. If you love to read, tutoring an adult literacy group could be a meaningful way of giving back; or your love of four-legged creatures may make you the perfect humane society ambassador. Ponder the topics that get you all revved up: advocacy, homelessness, AIDS, mental health, poverty, child abuse, disease, eating disorders, substance abuse, women's issues. Whatever your interest, begin taking steps to get involved in that area. And remember that if you make an obligation, stand by it. Organizations rely on their volunteers. Just because you aren't getting paid for your work doesn't mean people aren't counting on you.

Tranquil Tip: Help the drowning polar bears whose icecaps are melting and leaving them homeless! Global warming effects are all around us. Do your part to help save our cute furry friends and human ones, too. Join the virtual march against global warming at stopglobalwarming.org.

A Fusion of Fashion and Passion

Tired of running around town in leggings and T-shirts, I launched a line of yoga wear that would support jobs in the United States and give back to the community. I started working with bamboo fabric because it is sustainable (it exploits natural resources without destroying the ecological balance of a particular area), it wicks moisture (great for yoga and late-night dancing too!), is soft as cashmere, and doesn't pill. A portion of the proceeds from the clothing line goes to My Sister's Place—a local organization working to eradicate domestic violence. Basically, purchasing TranquiliT helps support a home-based seamstress in Ohio, abused women, and eco-friendly fabrics—all important to overall promotion of tranquility in our society.

Mentoring maven: Be a source of inspiration to others. Taking time out of your busy schedule to share your knowledge and expertise through tutoring, speaking, offering a mentoring program, or being a mentor to an up-and-coming colleague can have amazing karmic rewards. Oftentimes you can serve as a mentor simply by example. Let your life be a story that will affect others for years to come.

Host a ChariTea: If you love to entertain in a simple, yet chic way, combine a cause with this signature soirée. Invite all the acquaintances you can muster in one quaint space, and request that they bring a minimum nominal donation to the charity you have chosen (or offer them a choice of charities). The tea theme fits nicely with the charity focus and offers you a more casual setting and a less expensive time of day if you are renting space. Set the stage with fair trade tea, a testimonial about the cause close to your heart, simple savory cucumber and egg salad sandwiches, flowers donated by a local shop,

> Being an activist is the rent we
> pay for being on the planet.
> —ALICE WALKER

scones and butter cookies, and a mish-mash of china teacups from the neighborhood flea market. Give goody bags to all who attend with more info on how to get involved in the charity. A ChariTea is the perfect way to spend an afternoon blending your passionate palate with consciousness-raising for a cause close to your heart. Toolkit for putting this event together on p. 159.

Tranquil Tip: Another way to raise more revenue for a charity is to offer a raffle or silent auction. Request that your fave boutiques, yoga studios, and personal care services donate a product or service to the cause that participants can bid on or buy raffle tickets for, and watch the revenues go up for your charity! This is a win-win because your local hot spots support your efforts and they get their name out, the participants have the opportunity to walk away with great goodies while giving money to a worthy cause, and everyone benefits from the great karma of a fun event!

Gift giving gone global: Consider alternative gift giving, especially for those folks who truly do have everything they need. The idea behind alternative gift giving is that you donate an amount of money to a particular cause in someone's honor. For example, $20 buys wool for a weaver in Bosnia. As a gift to your favorite teacher, consider a gift of textbooks for a girl in need. At www.heifer.org you can buy a goat, flock of geese or ducks, honeybees, a llama, heifer, or even a water buffalo as a gift for families around the world in the name of your special someone. What an amazing way for a hip tranquil chick to put her values to her purchases!

Volunteer: With all that is happening around us, there are numerous ways to help nurture and support fellow human beings (and animals, too!). How about offering to volunteer locally with a group of friends to assist those in need? Count your blessings, nurture your friendships, and do great things together. Doing what you can to support those suffering is sure to help bring about conscious connections.

There are countless opportunities to give back. Take a volunteer vacation where you clean up after a natural disaster, build homes, or count whales. Go on a volunteer sabbatical and join the Peace Corps. I've heard nothing but glowing reviews from women who have carved out space in their life for such an experience. Or go local and find a nearby volunteerism umbrella organization and choose different offerings from their calendar of events—try an environmental activity by working in a community garden or going on a day hike in nearby mountains with a group of inner-city kids.

Tranquil Tip: When considering volunteer opportunities, it's important to find the right fit. Make sure you're comfortable with the group, the organization, and even the surroundings. A girlfriend signed up to help tutor homeless children, but didn't feel safe in the neighborhood where the tutoring was held and began to dread going. If she'd done the research up-front, she would have understood what she was getting into.

Go Abroad
Women for Women International has an online boutique filled with handmade pieces—beautiful jewelry, accessories, and household items made from women in conflict regions. A girlfriend found placemats made in Rwanda and a Nigerian apron to give to a friend who loves to cook. Rather than buy the latest perfectly proportioned Barbie, try **Ten Thousand Villages** for fun and interesting toys and gifts that teach children about the world and other cultures.

Be a good citizen: Share your voice and honor our foremothers who helped deliver the right to vote! Reading the paper or watching the news may be difficult to fit into an already tight schedule, but find some type of outlet that will keep you abreast of what is happening around you. And do your share to contribute to your community. If you have a small patch of grass in front of your city apartment, plant pansies or a small English boxwood. Pick up trash when you walk past a mess on the street. Sweep your sidewalk—and why not your neighbor's, too?

Give back: Explore ways to give back as a business owner, local shopper, or everyday citizen. The options are endless and the rewards are immeasurable. Throughout Tranquil Space's history, I've wanted my business efforts to benefit others beyond the practice of yoga and have chosen charities to ensure this happens. We continue to donate a portion of proceeds from all boutique sales to stopping domestic violence.

Fill a need: There are things around you every day that can benefit from your initiative. If your office doesn't recycle, gather the information on how to get started and request a meeting with the decision maker to present the data. Get creative by reusing paper when printing drafts or personal memos. Does your community lack a volunteer coordination system? Call local community centers, assisted living centers, museums, or nonprofits to see how volunteers could assist and whom they would need to contact, and put together an online blog catered to your community. When you see something missing in your community, get the ball rolling as the pioneer of the movement. Let your actions leave a legacy.

Creative Charity

Every few months at Tranquil Space, we plant a tree for every class pass purchased through the **Arbor Day Foundation.** This is our way to help yogis far and wide breathe better. We hold an annual "doga in the park," with dogs running wild and people doing yoga, to help raise awareness for the **local humane society** and also donate a portion of our bottled water sales to them. Annually we hold a holiday trunk show featuring local designers and donate a portion of our proceeds from the event to the **Fund for Women Artists,** which helps support women creating art—a perfect mix of charity and creativity!

Little Things Matter

Being socially conscious is a state of mind. Practice it in all situations. Smile at people as you walk by them. Say thank you. Sincerely compliment an outfit or haircut. Ask your colleague how she is and mean it. Help somebody who looks in need of assistance by holding the door, or giving directions to a disoriented passerby. Interacting with others in a respectful and reverent way is a sort of community "tax" for being in society.

Be involved with where you live and support its development by your everyday choices. Make an effort once a week to try a new local restaurant or store. You may get a thrill from a Broadway show, but imagine the joy of seeing a local play by a neighbor. If you own a business or manage a team, encourage your staff to volunteer and compensate them for their time doing so.

Going Green, Girl

Each day we must honor the earth and our surroundings. The air we breathe fills us with life. Recognize how your choices affect the environment. Here are some ideas on ways to add a bit more green into your everyday wardrobe of choices.

Live consciously: Live your values and share with others by example. • Wear sweatshop-free clothing made of organic cotton or bamboo. • Use water-saver faucets, showerheads, and toilets. • Drive a greener car such as a Toyota Prius or Honda Civic Hybrid, or go further and carpool, bike, walk, or take the bus to work or school. • Compost waste and put it into your garden. • Recycle personal products—make things last by altering hemlines and buttons to be more "in the now," donating to charity, or giving to friends. • Avoid excess packaging when purchasing and gift giving—a good percentage of our municipal solid waste stream is the result of unnecessary packaging. • Plant a Japanese red maple or even a baby fern to "green" your surroundings and help others breathe

> You have to hold yourself accountable for your actions, and that's how we're going to protect the Earth.
> —Julia Butterfly Hill

Chic and Green Cleaning Recipes

Use refillable bottles and make your own cleaning products, which will be nontoxic and best of all, inexpensive. **Vinegar** is a great natural cleaning product, disinfectant, and deodorizer. To create this concoction, mix 1 cup water to 1 cup vinegar in a spray bottle. Always test on an inconspicuous area. It is very economical and safe to use on most surfaces. Don't worry, the smell disappears when it dries. Use it on the bathtub, toilet, sink, and countertops in the bathroom; the stovetop, appliances, countertops, and floor in the kitchen; and in the washer as a natural fabric softener for your accoutrements. Great for us girls with sensitive skin. Add 1/2 cup of vinegar to the rinse cycle in place of store-bought fabric softener. Additional all-natural cleaning products include (1) **baking soda,** which cleans, deodorizes, softens water, scours, (2) **unscented soap,** which is biodegradable in liquid form, flakes, powders, and bars, and (3) **lemons,** which can be cut in half and sprinkled with baking soda on the cut section, then used to scrub dishes, surfaces, and stains.

by the Forest Stewardship Council (FSC)—it promotes responsible management of the world's forests. • Buying local supports your local economy and reduces the energy consumption required by the global transport of goods. • Try purchasing only necessities for a week.

Expand Your Vision

The paths to savvy social consciousness are many, and yours is a unique footprint. Maybe you have visions of joining the Peace Corps or helping build homes in Haiti, or planting a small community garden space in the city. Whatever it is, personalize it, ensure it reflects your values, and take action. View your resources as powerful forces for doing good and making a difference. Incorporate this notion every time you step onto the mat by dedicating your yoga practice as a way to serve the world.

In order to be savvy and socially conscious, explore ways to communicate your passions through activist efforts that exude your signature style. Share your knowledge

better. • Plan your day—do all your errands at once to reduce excessive driving.

Buy wisely: Reconsider how you spend your money and let this energy exchange reflect your yogic values, namely *ahimsa*. • Look for fair trade and organic coffee and tea as well as chocolate and bananas. • Buy recycled, chlorine-free and tree-free paper with the highest percentage of "postconsumer waste" (PCW). • Shop for local and organic food at farmers' markets near you. (Those berries flown in from Chile leave a footprint on the environment) • Buy organic, nontoxic, personal care products such as Burt's Bees, Jason's, Kiss My Face, Dr. Bronner's and Tom's of Maine. • Burn long-lasting light bulbs. • Shop for sustainably harvested seafood with the Marine Stewardship Council (MSC) logo that promotes responsible fishing practices. • Buy rechargeable batteries. • Look for energy-efficient appliances with the Energy Star logo. • Buy less-toxic paint. • Shop for wood products certified

> Two roads diverged in a
> wood, and I—I took the one
> less traveled by, and that has
> made all the difference.
> —ROBERT FROST

and expertise with the world by speaking, volunteering, or starting an online community. Recognize the interconnectedness of all beings by being mindful of how your actions affect the world. Time and money are valuable commodities. Choose wisely. Namaste.

Omwork

Explore your retail-therapy habits. Consider shopping at secondhand shops, with local independent designers and farmers, and find ways to make a difference with your shopping dollar. Reflect on your habits and review ways to begin putting your values to work when buying the latest gadget or succulent blueberry.

Incorporate new ways to make a difference. Which ideas appealed to you in this chapter? Can you begin making some small changes in certain areas? What small step are you willing to take now?

Get out there and make a difference. Host a ChariTea soirée (toolkit on p. 159), plant a community garden, become a Big Sister, participate in local elections, rallies, and protests—let your voice be heard. Consider Meals on Wheels, American Red Cross, Rotary international, Sierra Club, The Nature Conservancy, Special Olympics, or Habitat for Humanity. The options for excelling as a do-good diva are limitless.

Savvy Sources

Read

The Power of Purpose: Living Well by Doing Good, by Peter S. Temes

The Giving Tree, by Shel Silverstein

The Simple Living Guide: A Sourcebook for Less Stressful, More Joyful Living, by Janet Luhrs

Green Clean: The Environmentally Sound Guide to Cleaning Your Home, by Linda Mason Hunter and Mikki Halpin

Real Simple magazine

Organic Gardening magazine

Natural Home magazine

Visit

www.globalexchange.org

www.idealbite.org

www.newdream.org

www.sustainabletable.org

www.eco-labels.org

www.eco-chick.com

Listen

Knuckle Down, by Ani DiFranco

Songs from the Front Porch: An Acoustic Collection, by Michael Franti

The Very Best of UB40 1980–2000, by UB40

Where You Live, by Tracy Chapman

Global Soul, by Putumayo Presents

Tiempos, by Rubén Blades

Legend, by Bob Marley

—

Hip Tranquil Chick
Signature ChariTea Soirée

Gather a group of your fave fabulous women together to inspire, encourage, and motivate you on your hip and tranquil journey. Download the *Hip Tranquil Chick Signature ChariTea Soirée Toolkit* at www.hiptranquilchick.com to help you host the perfect soirée while diving into the concepts of *Hip Tranquil Chick*. Your signature soirée may be a one-time event or an ongoing session diving into each of the 12 chapters. This complimentary comprehensive guide includes:

- A greeting from Kimberly
- Planning guide
- Chic invites
- *Hip Tranquil Chick* discussion tips

- Savvy tips for the stylish chick
- Insight on how to create community at your fête
- Yoga sequence sheet
- Tasty treat and bubbly beve recipes
- Ideas on celebrating this movement in a socially conscious way
- And more!

Send your favorite signature soirée photos to Kimberly@hiptranquilchick. com to share them with our vibrant cyber community. Stay virtually connected with your hip tranquil chick community at www.hiptranquilchick.com/blog.

Acknowledgments

This book is a culmination of many years of living the hip tranquil chick lifestyle, and I have many peeps to thank for living it with me, teaching me along the way, letting me teach them, and ultimately supporting me during the process. Oodles of gratitude go out, in no particular order, to:

Tranquil Space Team, I am blessed with an amazing group of studio assistants, teachers, managers, advisory board, and consultants, without whom the growth of Tranquil Space, voted the best yoga studio in D.C., would not have been possible.

Tim Mooney, where do I begin? This man puts up with a girlfriend who has to schedule "date days" up to six months in advance. His patience, support, and ability to keep Louis occupied while I wrote is worth its weight in gold. I love you.

Linda Wilson, who gave birth to me, has smiled through my numerous nonconventional decisions since then, and who is one of my biggest fans.

Pops, who kept me up during childhood while pounding away on his typewriter, for encouraging the use of deductive reasoning, and for being my cheerleader throughout the writing process.

Gina Davis Kelley, my incredible studio director, who held down the fort so that I could write this book and has given me numerous giggles along the way.

Heather Haines, my long-lost sorority sister who graciously read this manuscript and provided very hip feedback.

Danielle and Anne, for clear and concise editing of the yoga poses.

Podcast listeners and blog readers, I owe you all many thanks for reading, listening, asking questions, offering suggestions, and helping build awareness of all things hip and tranquil. You rock!

Creativity circle, retreat, class, and workshop participants, I've learned so much from you over the years and am incredible grateful for your loyalty throughout my evolutionary creative process.

My teachers—from school to ballet to yoga. You have inspired me to do more than I dreamed possible.

Alma Bune, my incredibly insightful editor who was gratifyingly responsive and got hip tranquil chick from the start.

Katie McMillan and the Inner Ocean team, my publicist and publishing house have been more supportive than I could have ever dreamed!

Jennifer Gates, my amazing agent, who had as much enthusiasm for this project as I did. An impressive and ingenious gem.

Louis, my baby black pug, who has been a source of laughter and joy since he walked into my life one very special Christmas.

Morgan Johnson, a very talented illustrator who brought the hip tranquil chick to life.

Lillian Couch, my kick-ass 93-year-old Gramma who communicates via e-mail and has always served as an example of the ultimate chick!

Kevin and Susan Turnock, my fave couple from the country who supported me emotionally along the way and gave great insights.

Norissa Giangola, what an enthusiastic and hip chick! Thanks for coming into my life.

Elizabeth Falk, thank you for being the greening goddess.

Brian Winterfeldt, my dear friend who helped coin the concept hip tranquil chick.

Katharine Tillman, my assistant for almost two years who shared a passion for Anaïs Nin, Tori Amos, boys, and all things literary.

Jennifer Haile, a hip tranquil chick who has offered amazing support since she stepped foot into Tranquil Space.

Carole Sargent, my writing coach from the early days. You offered incredible insights into the world of publishing and encouraged me even though I had no idea what I wanted to write.

The talented who's who of hip tranquil chickness, **Lauren, Lisa, Gina, Rachael, Kate, Erin, Isabel, Kathy,** and **Susan.**

Elmer Ewing, my statuesque grandpa who escaped to heaven when I was six but whose memory has never left. I love you.

The brilliant hip tranquil chick feedback crew who gave valuable insights into what was missing in the world of hip and tranquil chick lit. You know who you are.

Lauren Brownstein, my dearest co-hip hop class diva who supported this book in its varied stages from first mention.

Doug Morris, a fellow author who lended support and encouragement at the start of a long literary journey.

About the Author

Kimberly Wilson has a master's degree in women's studies and is a self-diagnosed bibliophile whose heart begins to race when she steps a kitten heel into any bookstore. Her creation of Tranquil Space yoga and TranquiliT luxe lifestyle wear—along with her charity-focused soirées and midwest charm—have been featured in numerous media outlets, including *Martha Stewart Living Radio, DailyCandy, Lucky,* and the *Washington Post.* She lives in a cozy raspberry and leopard-print-embellished condo in D.C.'s artsy Dupont Circle with Louis the pug and two felines named after French impressionists. Kimberly enjoys musing in her blog and podcast.

Join the hip tranquil chick movement at *hiptranquilchick.com.*

Amy Mullarkey

Tranquil Space® was voted Washington, D.C.'s best yoga studio. This vinyasa yoga playground in the heart of Dupont Circle offers more than 40 creative classes in two sunny studios each week. Sip tea, shop our TranquiliT Boutique, indulge in our specialty spa treatments, or simply let go through a nurturing yoga practice. We have additional studios in Bethesda, Maryland, and downtown D.C. Join us and uncover your own tranquil space within, both on and off the yoga mat. For more information, visit www.tranquilspace.com.

Joshua Cogan

As seen in *Shape*, *DailyCandy*, and *Lucky*, TranquiliT® luxe lifestyle wear is perfect for yoga and beyond. **The TranquiliT collection** transitions easily from workout wear to around-the-town flair—from the yoga mat to the market or museum. The fabric is lush bamboo and organic cotton which moves with and flatters the body. After spending years running around town in leggings and T-shirts, Kimberly craved a more stylish approach to an active lifestyle. TranquiliT offers a trendy alternative to traditional workout wear and assists the active fashionista in expressing her personal style. For more information, visit www.tranquilit.com.

Joshua Cogan

Hip Tranquil Chick is not simply a book, but a movement for bringing all things hip and tranquil into the limelight of the modern girl's bustling life. **Hip Tranquil Ventures**™ offers business and lifestyle mentoring, yoga and creativity workshops and retreats, sassy speaking, must-have lifestyle literature, and audio CDs—all catered to those seeking a mindfully extravagant life. For all sorts of scoop, visit www.hiptranquilchick.com.

Tranquil Space Foundation™ is a non-profit community dedicated to helping create a tranquil space within our society through the donation of time, yoga, and resources to those in need of a dose of tranquility. Learn more about our signature program that blends yoga, leadership, and creativity for young women. For more information, visit www.tranquilspacefoundation.org.